SOMME
1916

SOMME
1916

ANDREW ROBERTSHAW

DUNDURN
TORONTO

Visit us at
Dundurn.com | @dundurnpress | Facebook.com/dundurnpress
Pinterest/dundurnpress

Dundurn
3 Church Street, Suite 500
Toronto, Ontario, Canada
M5E 1M2

CONTENTS

INTRODUCTION

In popular imagination, the Battle of the Somme of 1916 can be summed up in a single word: 'disaster'. Time after time journalists, amateur historians and members of the public make reference to 1 July, the supposed first day of the battle, as the 'worst day in the history of the British army'. The media have a habit of referring to the figure of '60,000 dead' on this day; in fact, there were 57,000 'casualties' – prisoners, wounded, missing and dead. There is no disputing that these are terrible figures, quite impossible to imagine in the twenty-first century. However, they resulted from a political decision taken by the British government to commit an army to France and possibly Belgium in the event of war against Germany. The inevitable consequence of this was that the British army, the British Expeditionary Force, would fight shoulder to shoulder with the conscript armies of its ally France against a more numerous German force. Only a swift victory could offer the possibility of limited casualties, but the war was not 'over by Christmas'. As an increasingly large force of British and imperial troops was committed to the Western Front their casualties continued to rise. Unlike the Second World War, in which the British army faced Nazi Germany for a few weeks before Dunkirk and then for less than a year after D Day, the BEF faced its main enemy, Imperial Germany, during the entire period from August 1914 to 11 November 1918. Men were killed and wounded every day, even when no battles were being fought. In these circumstances, as the BEF rose in strength to millions, daily 'wastage' was numbered in hundreds or thousands. One way of limiting this statistic was to mount an offensive that would end the war: peace would stop the dying though achieving this would doom many to death on the battlefield. The only other solution was negotiation, but the politicians of neither side chose this option. It was left to the military commanders to plan and execute the battles that would bring about the victory that would end the war. This inevitably led to the Somme and the other battles that would follow.

However, fighting battles with millions of soldiers, with new weapons, tactics and ways of warfare, the generals faced new challenges and the possibility that their mistakes would lead to the deaths of sons, fathers and brothers at a rate never seen before. Some talk about the 'butchery of the Somme', and Douglas Haig as chief butcher, without ever considering that casualties were inevitable. No general fought a battle in the Great War without heavy casualties and even the much-vaunted German 'Stormtroopers' ultimately failed amid staggering losses. The basic arithmetic of the Great War indicates that the German army suffered the heaviest losses, then the French and then the BEF. In other words, it was 'safer' to be in the BEF under Haig than to be commanded by Ludendorff. These figures are all relative, but the men who fought on the Somme felt that they were doing the right thing and did not have the benefit of our hindsight.

Since 1916, hundreds of books have been written about the battle. I have written one myself, and there is no doubt that more will follow. We must be mindful to distinguish between historical 'facts' and their interpretation, otherwise a single volume on the Somme would have already proved to be sufficient. What I intend to do in this publication is put the events of 1916 in their historical perspective, to present the facts of the battle and to provide my interpretation of the events of 100 years ago. Not everyone will agree with my views, nor with those of any other historian who risks his or her reputation in the pursuit of understanding past events.

I have spent over thirty years providing audiences with a range of presentations and lectures on the Great War, taken part in numerous archaeological projects on the Western Front and appeared in television documentaries on the subject. I have spent months on the

Somme in all conditions and met old soldiers and their relatives in the locations they served. Of greater significance, to me at least, is that my grandfather served on the Somme as a private, survived the war, though wounded three times between 1916 and 1919, and came home to raise a family. In common with many old soldiers, he did not speak freely with his wife or son about his experiences. He did, however, pass judgement on the generals who commanded the men on the Somme and subsequently. When given a copy of Alan Clark's *The Donkeys* on its publication, a book highly critical of the British generalship, he read it and returned it to my father with a brief comment: 'I don't agree. The generals did their job; we did ours. We won!' To put this in perspective, my grandfather John Andrew Robertshaw was a grammar school boy who volunteered with the father of Ted Hughes, the future poet. When asked why he was so keen to volunteer in 1914, he told my father '*To get the uniform off*'. By that he meant to go to war, beat Imperial Germany and come home, at which point he could 'Get the uniform off'. Knowing what we do about the Great War and subsequent events, these comments might appear at variance with received wisdom about that first conflict of the twentieth century. If this is the case, I am gratified. As the saying goes 'The past is a foreign country; they do things differently there'. My grandfather did his job well and I see him today as a 'victor' not a 'victim'. If he was let down by anyone it was the politicians who failed to avoid the next world catastrophe just twenty-one years later.

TIMELINE

1914

28 June	Assassination of Franz Ferdinand in Sarajevo
28 July	Austria declares war on Serbia
29 July	Russia mobilises
1 August	Germany declares war on Russia
3 August	German invasion of Belgium
4 August	Britain enters the war
4–19 August	BEF mobilised
23–24 August	The BEF is involved in the Battle of Mons
26 August	Battle of Le Cateau – successful rear guard action by BEF II Corps
7–10 September	Battle of the Marne – German advance halted
12–15 September	Battle of the Aisne – German army goes on the defensive
4–10 October	Unsuccessful defence of Antwerp by Royal Naval Division
19–22 October	First Battle of Ypres – British, French and Belgian forces prevent capture of Ypres
	Western Front stabilised

1915

10–13 March	Battle of Neuve-Chapelle – BEF's first offensive
22 April–25 May	Second Battle of Ypres – first German use of chlorine gas
7 May	RMS *Lusitania* sunk by a German submarine off Ireland
25 September–8 October	Battle of Loos – first use of gas by the BEF
19 December	General Sir Douglas Haig takes over as Commander-in-Chief of the BEF from Field Marshal Sir John French
29 December	Haig attends conference to discuss Anglo-French offensive on a 60-mile front on the Somme

1916

24 January	First Military Service Act passed by the House of Commons (conscription of unmarried men aged 18–41)
21 February	Battle of Verdun begins
12 March	Allied military conference at Chantilly regarding summer offensive
14 April	Lord Kitchener informs Haig that the British cabinet had agreed that the war could only be ended in battle
1 May	General Pétain receives command of the group of French Armies of the Centre. General Nivelle takes command of French 2nd Army
21 May	German attack on Vimy Ridge
25 May	Conscription extended to include married men aged 18–41
31 May	Battle of Jutland
4 June	Russian Brusilov Offensive against Austro-Hungarian and German forces
5 June	Death of Field Marshal Earl Kitchener in the sinking of HMS *Hampshire* en route to Russia to discuss joint strategy

1916

24 June	Preliminary bombardment on the Somme begins (British code: 'U Day'; final day to be 'Z Day')
27 June	Haig moves his headquarters to the Château Valvion, 12 miles from Albert; 'X Day'
28 June	'Y Day'; Z Day postponed by two days due to bad weather
29 June	'Y+1'
30 June	'Y+2'
1 July	'Z Day' – attack at 7.30 a.m. Greenwich Mean Time
15–22 September	Battle of Flers-Courcelette; first use of tanks
13–18 November	Battle of the Ancre; Beaumont-Hamel captured
18 November	Official end of the Battle of the Somme

HISTORICAL BACKGROUND

By the spring of 1916, the Great War had been in progress for over eighteen months and the Western Front was a stalemate. German, French, Belgian and British troops faced each other over 'no-man's-land' from trenches that stretched from the dunes of the Belgian coast to the Swiss border. Hundreds of thousands of men had already become casualties and their loss was a factor in ensuring that the war would not be resolved by negotiation. It had all started very differently. At the outbreak of war in August 1914, Germany and her ally Austria-Hungary faced war against the Triple Entente of France, Russian and Britain. To deal with this threat the Imperial German army intended to mobilise rapidly, invade France and capture Paris, as they had done in Franco-Prussian War (1870–71), and then turn east to confront the massive Russian army, which would take time to mobilise and enter the war effectively.

The German plan was the brainchild of General Alfred von Schlieffen and called for an invasion of France through neutral Belgium, outflanking the main French border defences. This might bring Britain into the war, as there was an international agreement to guarantee the neutrality of that small country, but the British Expeditionary Force (BEF) was smaller than the armies of Belgium and even Switzerland, and was regarded as insignificant in German planning. When the BEF arrived in France in mid-August it was added

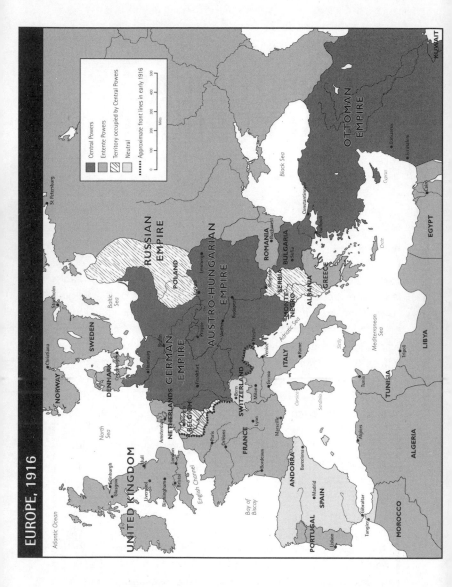

EUROPE, 1916

Central Powers
Entente Powers
Territory occupied by Central Powers
Neutral
Approximate front lines in early 1916

to the left wing of the French forces facing the German border. This put the British troops in the path of the German advance as it reached Mons near Brussels on 23 August, only three weeks after the war had begun. The BEF was pushed back and retreated with its French allies to the gates of Paris. French attacks in the south to regain the territories of Alsace and Lorraine, lost to Germany in 1871, had failed and casualties in the 'Battle for the Borders' were mounting.

At this point and with victory within reach, the German commanders realised that the number of men available to them was insufficient to complete the task. To complicate matters, German supply lines, along which came rations, ammunition and fodder for the horses, were now overstretched. The French and Belgian railway networks had been destroyed both by design and in the fighting. Everything upon which the German forces depended was being brought to the front from the German border by horse-drawn vehicles. The situation was impossible and the Germans faced collapse unless it changed. Worse still, Russia was mobilising faster than expected and Berlin was facing the real possibility of attack by the Russian 'steamroller'. The only way that the Germans could hold on to the territory they had captured in France and Belgium and still have troops available to face the threat from the east was to 'dig-in'. They went from offence to defence as it takes fewer troops to hold ground than to attack. In addition, trenches with barbed wire and well-sited machine guns and artillery greatly increase the ability of the garrison to resist enemy assaults.

FROM COLOUR TO CAMOUFLAGE

The French infantry went to war in blue uniforms with red trousers and some of the cavalry wore breastplates and helmets as if they were at Waterloo in 1815. Although some shiny pieces of equipment were covered, there was no attempt at camouflage. The results in the opening days of the war were predictable. By 1915, the French army had adopted a 'horizon blue' uniform better suited to the new warfare.

Trenches were constructed first in the area where the opposing forces found themselves in September and the line was extended north to the Belgian coast as both sides fought to capture or hold on to as much territory as possible during October and November. By Christmas 1914, no-man's-land stretched along a line of trenches from Switzerland to the North Sea. The German forces had mauled the Russian army and, although they were now engaged in fighting similar to that taking place on the Western Front, it appeared possible that a victory in the east would free up the troops needed to complete a successful campaign in the west. The only question was when. By the new year of 1915 the French army alone had lost nearly half a million men, killed, wounded and prisoners, but her soldiers, like Belgium's, were motivated by the fact that the war was being fought on their soil. French, Belgian and British politicians instructed their generals not to give up an inch of ground. This meant that while the Germans could select the most tactically useful position, withdrawing to higher ground where possible, Allied commanders had to occupy areas that were military 'death traps' for political reasons. The area held by the Allies around the Belgian city of Ypres formed a crescent, or salient, that stuck out into German-held territory. Their forces on higher ground could dominate the German troops below them, and the politicians turned down all appeals to abandon this potential 'killing zone'. By the end of the war, the Allies had suffered 400,000 casualties in this area alone.

Both sides had broadly similar weapons, once they were entrenched, and mounting attacks from behind increasingly deep belts of barbed wire would inevitably be costly. Even if local successes were achieved, the depth of the trench system meant that as attackers broke through the successive lines of defence, a process that took time, the defenders could divert reinforcements to the sector under attack. In these circumstances, the initial onrush of an offensive could be likened to throwing a bucket of water across a carpet. The defenders simply absorbed the attack and the attackers ran out of impetus. Nonetheless, both sides hoped that new tactics and weapons would prove to be the 'war winning' combination.

Kaiser Wilhelm II saw himself as a great military leader able to assure Germany a rapid and decisive victory. (Author's collection)

'The Reservist's song'. The German army greatly increased the size of its forces by mobilising its reserves in addition to the regular forces. (Author's collection)

BRITANNIA RULES THE WAVES

When it was mobilised in August 1914, the BEF arrived on the continent without the loss of a single ship or man because the Royal Navy were able to prevent attacks on the shipping routes across the Channel.

As the war entered a stalemate on the Western Front – a name coined by the Germans to reflect the fact that they were fighting on two fronts – Allied politicians and generals looked for ways to bring the war to a successful conclusion. Whilst most of the military favoured putting more resources and manpower into the effort on the Western Front, others advocated indirect approaches. One option was to take the war elsewhere, away from mainland Europe, effectively using a 'backdoor' to victory by mounting a campaign that would provide an 'eastern' front. By 1915 Italy had joined the Allied cause and military resources were provided to ensure that her forces could draw Austro-Hungarian, and later German, troops to the Italian front. Turkey's decision to join Germany and Austria-Hungary against the Triple Entente offered an alternative theatre of operation in the east. With the backing of both the French and British governments, a combined force was sent to Turkey with the overall intention of forcing the Turkish to capitulate and providing a sea route to Russia via the Mediterranean and Dardanelles. The Gallipoli campaign, which began in April 1915, was a military and naval failure. Instead of a quick victory opening a route to Russia, the Allies became involved in a trench stalemate similar to the Western Front. The Turkish army proved to be a formidable enemy and as casualties mounted in January 1916 the enterprise was abandoned and the forces evacuated.

In the spring of 1915 both sides had attempted to mount offensives on the Western Front in the hope of achieving some form of breakthrough. The Battle of Neuve-Chapelle (10–13 March 1915) had demonstrated the limitations of artillery and infantry, especially when poor communication meant that reserves were late in arriving to exploit a breakthrough. This was countered by a much more ambitious attack at Ypres on 22 April when German troops used chlorine gas to poison the French, Canadian and British defenders. Despite early success, the battle was not decisive and although German lines moved closer to the battered city of Ypres, it did not fall and the war continued. A subsequent British attack in early May at Aubers Ridge was a failure. French forces were not to be denied their chance to mount an offensive either. The Second Battle of Artois in late May saw French colonial troops attempt to capture Vimy Ridge having already pushed back the German lines by a matter of miles. Further south some of the frontline of 1 July 1916 was established by a French attack near Hébuterne in June, which captured a good deal of ground on the northern Somme.

Britain's greatest effort of 1915 came at Loos where a large-scale Franco-British offensive action using gas in retaliation for the Ypres attack was mounted on 25 September. By 1915, the arrival of British Territorial Force units and the first of the 'New Army' volunteers meant that the British army was rapidly expanding. Nevertheless, the BEF was tiny in comparison with the forces available to France. The French military, politicians and public were looking to the British to play an increasingly major part in the war and take at least some of the burden from France's forces whose casualties dwarfed those of her ally. The

In answer to Lord Kitchener's appeal for troops to bolster the tiny BEF, hundreds of thousands of British civilians enlisted in the early part of the war. Equipping, arming and training these men would take time. (IWM MU37016)

battle at Loos, referred to as 'The Big Push', was preceded by a large-scale bombardment and the British 1st Army had hopes of victory. There were plans to push cavalry through the gap created by the artillery and infantry and some spoke of possibly capturing the major city of Lille and an advance on Mons, in Belgium. The early morning attack was initially successful and, despite heavy casualties, the British managed to force their way deep into German territory between Loos and La Bassée. However, once again there were problems with sending reinforcements forward, and many senior officers were lost acting as unit commanders since their telephone communications failed, cut by enemy shellfire, and they were forced to take command of the men around them. The majority were sniped as they led men forward. To complicate matters further, German tactics called for counter-attacks on any position lost to enemy assault. In consequence, the see-saw battle went on until mid-October, when it was clear that neither side could achieve anything more.

With the failure of the 'eastern' approach to unlocking the stalemate, it was clear that only a direct solution on the Western Front would provide the Allies with a decisive victory. This would clearly be costly in terms of resources and human life, but the only other option was negotiation. The politicians of France and Britain would not consider this approach. Their conclusion was that the armies of the principal combatants, in conjunction with that of their co-belligerent, Belgium, would have to mount an offensive. Indirect assistance would be sought from Russia and Italy, who could be requested to mount their own simultaneous offensives. This would tie down German and Austro-Hungarian forces, rendering them unable to transfer reserves to the Western Front to deal with the Franco-Belgian-British attack. The Western Front was an exhausting battle for the German forces. This war of attrition would also cost the lives of tens of thousands of Allied soldiers. However, at the time this policy was under discussion, thousands of men were being killed every month simply 'holding the line': an offensive that would end the war, possibly in a matter of months, offered a better outcome if seen in terms of the mathematics of war rather than the human cost of either approach.

Of course, the politicians could present the strategy, but it was left to the generals to put it into effect. The commander of the British

1st Army, Sir Douglas Haig, was highly critical of the manner in which his Commander-in-Chief, Sir John French, had handled the battle. He was especially concerned by the way in which the reserves had been kept too far back and then released too late to be effective. Haig was not alone in his opinion, and, under political and military pressure, he replaced Sir John French in December 1915. Five months earlier, the French Commander-in-Chief had proposed that all the Allies should co-ordinate their war effort, and a permanent committee was created to this end. In November 1915, after meetings between the Prime Ministers of France and Great Britain, a plan was drawn up for large-scale attacks by the forces of Britain, France, Italy and Russia in the late spring of 1916. For Britain and France, this meant that France and Flanders would be the main theatre of operation.

On 29 December 1915, just ten days after Haig had become Commander-in-Chief of the BEF, he attended a meeting with Joffre, General Foch, the French President, Prime Minister and other senior French politicians. There, General Haig was put under pressure to take over more of the frontline from the French army and to prepare for an offensive in conjunction with French forces north of the River Somme. This plan was subject to change and by January 1916 Joffre

was envisaging a number of alternative locations for the offensive, only one of which would be on the Somme. It was intended to occur in late April and on a front of at least 7 miles. Joffre considered this attack a means of wearing down enemy forces prior to the main thrust elsewhere. At the time Haig was looking at alternative plans of his own, specifically focusing on

Sir Douglas Haig, known to his senior officers as 'D.H.' and to the men as 'The Chief'. (IWM Q23659)

In February 1916 the German army began an offensive centred on the French fortress town of Verdun. The result of this battle was to increase pressure for an Allied offensive on the Somme. (IWM Q23760)

Belgium, where there were clear objectives, including the capture of ports from which German submarines were operating and the of cutting major rail lines supplying enemy forces in that area. By mid-February Joffre had abandoned his plans for the BEF to engage in a battle of attrition and it was agreed that the main effort later in the year would be an Anglo-French offensive on the Somme.

Although planning for this future operation had begun, on 21 February 1916 German forces made an unexpected and decisive attack on the fortress of Verdun. As both sides poured men into this battle it became clear that the offensive was not going to last a matter of days. French casualties mounted rapidly Joffre put Haig under pressure to take over yet more of the front and bring forward the planned Somme offensive. Approval for this plan was received from the British government in early April. However, the French forces' potential for large-scale involvement in the offensive was diminishing on a daily basis as staggering losses at Verdun drained away French reserves of manpower. At one point, it appeared as though the whole plan would be abandoned or that if an attack on the Somme were carried out it would be a purely British operation. It was certain

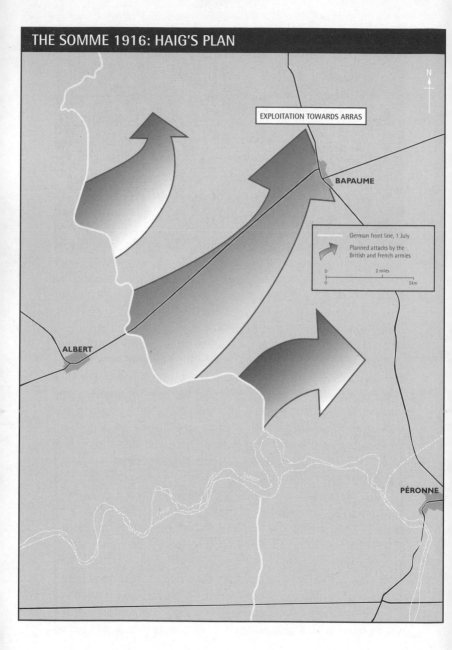

THE SOMME 1916: HAIG'S PLAN

EXPLOITATION TOWARDS ARRAS

BAPAUME

German front line, 1 July

Planned attacks by the
British and French armies

0   2 miles
0   5km

ALBERT

PÉRONNE

that in the light of Verdun the Somme offensive would not be the overwhelming Allied attack that had originally been envisaged. The British government had already been warned that under the prevailing circumstances they could not expect the decisive result that had been forecast. It was unfortunate that this fact could not be communicated to members of the public or the army. When the news of the 'Big Push' was revealed, many felt that it would be a decisive, perhaps knockout blow. The reality of the prevailing military situation made this doubtful and there were other complications for the BEF that made it unlikely that the Somme battle would be a war winner.

When a meeting was held on 31 May in the French President's railway car Haig met with Joffre and other senior French military and political leaders. The background to this meeting was a strongly held belief that Verdun would fall and the fact that some French politicians were against any form of offensive at all. Haig's response was simply to confirm that he had agreed an outline plan with Joffre and had the approval of his government; all he now needed was a date. This was set for 1 July to coincide with the Russian offensive on the Eastern Front. By mid-month Haig was under pressure from the French to bring this date forward, and agreed to 29 June. The scene was set for an attack by the largest British force that had ever taken the field at a time not chosen by the British commander, in a location that offered no clear military objective, with an army that was largely under-trained, if not untrained, and in the knowledge that success

THE MYSTERY OF THE MISSING

German soldiers were issued with zinc 'dog tags' for identification in case they became casualties. British identity discs were initially made of aluminum, but by 1915 'vulcanised fibre' was used instead. Only one tag was provided and, due to the sheer numbers of the dead on the Somme, the tags were recovered, but not the bodies. When, months later, the battlefields were cleared, the corpses of tens of thousands of British soldiers were discovered, but not identified by name. This explains many of the 'missing'.

British infantry wait in a shallow trench during the September 1916 fighting while a working party advances. Note the grave marker and tank in the distance. (Author's collection)

was unlikely. However, the offensive had British political backing and would, if successful, avoid the loss of Verdun and the resultant French political crisis. Importantly, it would allow the British government to demonstrate to her allies that its forces were fully committed to the common cause. These diplomatic objectives were about to commit hundreds of thousands of British soldiers to a battle in which the result was far from certain. In previous wars Britain had avoided committing large field armies, which it did not have, to the main theatre of operation. Instead she relied on a small field army and the power of an overwhelming navy to achieve the military results the government required. The agreement with France meant that Britain would for the first time in her history raise a mass citizen army to face Imperial Germany. After the butcher's bill of over 70,000 men killed and wounded at Borodino during a single day in 1812, when Napoleon's 500,000-strong force met the Russians at the gates of Moscow, Europe knew all about the cost of putting mass armies into battle. For Britain, which had relied upon an army that was in essence an 'Imperial police force', the consequences were inevitably going to be shocking, even if the battle was successful.

THE ARMIES

The Commanders

Lieutenant General Sir Henry Rawlinson (1864–1925)

Though it is believed that the senior commanders on the Somme were cavalrymen, Rawlinson was an infantryman who served in both the Rifles and Brigade of Guards. His early experience was in the numerous colonial struggles that characterised Queen Victoria's long and far from peaceful reign. Like Haig, he had served in both the Sudan and the Boer War. Whilst serving in the latter campaign as a column commander, and later after observing the Japanese army on manoeuvre, he was favourably impressed by the superiority of volunteer soldiers over conscripts and judged that massed machine guns were highly effective. At the same time, he concluded that infantry would decide 'the issue of battle' and that cavalry should be trained to fight on foot. Unfortunately, he ascribed the establishment of the trench system around Port Arthur in the Russo-Japanese War to the Japanese attackers' lack of initiative. In 1914, he was without command and was appointed Director of Recruiting by Kitchener, with whom he had served in the Sudan and South Africa. Rawlinson shared Kitchener's view that the war would not be 'over by Christmas' and that Britain would need to raise a citizen army.

Rawlinson served under Sir John French at the first Battle of Ypres in the autumn of 1914. Under Sir Douglas Haig, commander of 1st Army, he planned and executed the operation at Neuve-Chapelle. He concluded that artillery was the key to success and devoted lavish attention to the preparations for an ambitious bombardment. This included amassing an unprecedented amount of ammunition and artillery pieces and the use of innovative technology in the form of aerial photography. In subsequent operations he neglected artillery and, although he used other military innovations such as gas and smoke at Loos in September, there is a noticeable lack of consistency in his application of the lessons he learned. However, he assigned a New Army division to the capture of the village of Loos, demonstrating his faith in these newly raised formations. Having been given command of 4th Army in early 1916, Rawlinson devoted himself to planning the summer offensive, first near Ypres and later on the Somme. Once again, his performance was inconsistent as he abandoned large-scale plans to screen the attack with smoke, despite the advantage this technique offered at Loos, whilst at the same time reducing the employment of gas.

Haig chose Sir Henry Rawlinson as commander of 4th Army because of his experience as a subordinate commander and his ability to plan complex operations. He also had experience of working with the New Army troops that would form an important element of his command. Unfortunately, the two men disagreed fundamentally on the scope and 'pace' of the battle. Haig's preference to undertake an ambitious operation with minimum preliminary preparation that would make a bold thrust deep into enemy territory and pave the way for 'open', rather than trench, warfare, was at odds with Rawlinson's caution. Rawlinson's concept of 'bite and hold', using the artillery to screen the infantry and gradually eating into the enemy position, demonstrated caution. The operational plan that resulted was based on a series of compromises which, arguably, showed Rawlinson's failure to resist his superior's views and his poor leadership. Critically, when planning for the Somme battle, Rawlinson was inconsistent with tactical doctrine. He offered useful guidance for some aspects of the forthcoming battle, but largely left it to subordinate commanders to decide how to employ supporting artillery and even which tactics to use at battalion level to help them cross into the enemy position.

On the eve of the battle, Rawlinson wrote in his diary that he was 'pretty confident of success'. It remained to be seen whether that confidence would be enough.

General Sir Douglas Haig (1861–1928)

Sir Douglas Haig had a long and distinguished career before 1914. It began with the cavalry, serving first in the Sudan and then the Boer War (1899–1902). In the period after this conflict, he worked closely with Richard Haldane, the Secretary of State for War, to carry out a wide range of reforms necessary to improve the British army. He also worked with the British Indian army to reform its organisation and ability to mobilise. In 1914 he went to the continent as commander of 1st Corps of the BEF; by the following year he was the commander of 1st Army and by Christmas 1915 he had replaced Sir John French as Commander-in-Chief of the entire BEF. From his December meeting with Marshal Joffre, at which the significance of the presence of the French Prime Minister would not have been missed, Haig was trying to influence decisions even though he was a junior military partner in a coalition. His instruction from Kitchener, Secretary of State for War, was that his 'command is an independent one', even though he would have to co-operate with the Allies. Haig's initial view of the forthcoming battle was that it would be decisive if France and Britain could deliver sufficient force. His training and outlook suggested an ambitious plan of operation in which a breakthrough on the Somme would ultimately lead to victory. However, the events of the spring of 1916 meant that a decisive outcome became less likely. At the same time, the importance placed by the Allies, especially the French, on the contribution made by the BEF to the joint strategy became increasingly critical. The battle became known in the press as Haig's 'Big Push' and it was clear to him by the early summer of 1916 that this would be a mainly British battle, fought with inexperienced, if not under-trained troops. Haig warned Prime Minister Herbert Asquith that he did not have 'an army' in France, he had 'an army in training'. What he needed before the battle was more time for training. With the dates for a series of offensives already set by politicians, he was denied this opportunity to improve the chances of success. On the eve of battle, the military reality of the situation made this increasingly less likely. Haig wrote 'I feel that everything possible to achieve success has been done. But whether or not we are successful lies in the Power above.'

General Joseph Joffre (1852–1931)

Affectionately known as 'Papa', Joffre was French Commander-in-Chief throughout the Battle of the Somme. During 1914 he worked hard to ensure that there was no repeat of the disaster of 1870–71, when Paris fell and France was defeated. As commander in 1915 he planned the series of offensives designed to expel the German invaders from French soil, for which his only reward was a massive casualty list. This loss of life could not shake the resolve of the French to eject the German army and the battle Joffre planned on the Somme for the summer of 1916 was a 'wearing out fight' designed to break German resolve. Joffre was dismissive of Haig's concept of a rapid breakthrough achieved by a lightening barrage and surprise. He shared Rawlinson's view that the battle called for extensive use of artillery. The success achieved by French forces on both banks of the Somme on 1 July can be attributed to the number of guns, especially of larger calibres, that Joffre provided for his troops.

The British Commander-in-Chief Sir Douglas Haig with French generals Joffre and Foch in September 1916. He was made aware by Prime Minister Asquith that he was the junior partner in the coalition. The BEF had to play its part on the Western Front to assist its ally.

Although Joffre was without doubt the senior partner in the coalition, he was not the commander of the Allied forces. The independent commanders could not ignore him, but he acted only with their consent. This required diplomacy. During the Somme battle Joffre relied upon Ferdinand Foch, commander of the French Northern Army Group, to work with the British. To this end joint planning meetings of the senior British and French commander were held. If relations were at times strained in the period leading up to 1 July, Joffre avoided the problems that had beset General Sir John French's relationship with the French high command. Later in the campaign, Joffre and Haig did argue about strategy employed in the continued battle, but this did not prevent them working together in pursuit of their joint objective.

Generalleutnant Hermann von Stein (1854–1927)

General von Stein was the commander of XIV Reserve Corps, which was to face the British attack. He was a long-serving professional soldier and had risen from divisional commander to Quartermaster General on the outbreak of war. In September 1914, he became the commander of the Reserve Corps, which had just taken over the Somme sector. The troops commanded by von Stein proved to be innovative and daring, mounting ambitious raids against the French and latterly the British forces facing them. The corps was able to take the initiative on numerous occasions and the objective of 'dominating' no-man's-land, which British tactical doctrine demanded, was made almost impossible by these advanced German techniques. This was partly due to von Stein's leadership and in late February XIV Reserve Corps circulated a document on patrolling and trench raiding which was eventually sent to all main headquarters within the army. This document covered everything from intelligence and the choice of weapons to deception plans and the value of decorations to successful raiders. In short, it demonstrates the level of preparation achieved by the corps even before the first shell of the preliminary bombardment was fired. On 1 July, despite the weight of that preliminary bombardment and the number of men committed against his front, von Stein retained control of most of his forces and gave personal orders for some of the important counter-attacks.

General der Infanterie Fritz von Below (1853–1918)

General von Below commanded the German 2nd Army from his headquarters at Saint-Quentin. Despite making a series of proposals to higher command on how to deal with the growing threat of a British attack in his sector in spring 1916, von Below was largely ignored. In part, this was due to the prevailing attitude of German High Command to the British forces, especially the fighting abilities of the New Army units. In March 1916, von Below proposed an attack against the British before they could build up their forces for their own offensive. He was, however, working against the background of the Verdun operation, which was drawing in German troop reserves and munitions, both of which would be needed for his planned operation to succeed. His initial proposal ignored, von Below took matters into his own hands and was one of the architects of the extended trench, dugout and barbed wire system that was in place on 1 July. Despite thorough preparations, von Below was sufficiently concerned by 2 June to once again send a message to Erich von Falkenhayn about the still growing threat on the Somme. The Chief of Staff shared some of von Below's concerns and had already considered a number of schemes on the Western Front which appeared to have more potential than the Verdun battle, which was now four months old and not achieving its aims. However, two days after the request to launch a pre-emptive attack on the Somme, the surprise Russian 'Brusilov' offensive tore into the Austro-Hungarian forces on the Eastern Front. It was no longer possible to use reserve forces on any of the schemes considered for the Western Front: German units were sent east to help stem the Russian attack. By 1 July, despite all his calls for assistance, von Below had only received an additional four divisions of infantry and some heavy artillery. Judging by the scale of the threat facing him, von Below must have considered the situation far from ideal and must have been aware that the Allied war strategy was, at least as far as 2nd Army was concerned, producing results which threatened his own ability to deal with the offensive when it came on the Somme.

The Soldiers

British

On the outbreak of war, the armies of Britain, France and Germany were unequal in terms of size, experience and professionalism. France and Germany both used universal conscription and were capable of putting millions of men into the field. Britain relied on a purely volunteer force and could mobilise no more than 100,000 men of the BEF in August 1914. However, the level of individual training achieved by the men of the British army was probably superior to their continental allies and opponents. Importantly, Britain's senior officers and planners had the benefit of their experience of the Boer War and knew what a modern war could look like. Since the Boer War there had been dramatic changes in every aspect of the army, from mobile field artillery, to uniforms, field craft, rifles and marksmanship. What handicapped the BEF was its small size. The force that went to France in 1914 consisted of four, later six, divisions. Even when it was bolstered by the arrival of the Territorial Forces from October 1915, the British force was simply too small to make an effective contribution to the struggle.

A group of wartime volunteers of the Middlesex Regiment wearing the distinctive leather equipment given to men of the 'New Armies'. (Author's collection)

Lord Kitchener, who became Secretary of State for War in 1914, recognised that the conflict might be protracted and call for reserves of military manpower not currently available. His solution was to raise the 'New Armies', calling for hundreds of thousands of volunteers who would be trained and equipped for commitment to the war in Europe at such a time as they could make a decisive contribution. He foresaw this as being likely in 1917. Circumstances sent the 'New Armies' to France and Flanders in 1915 and they represented around half the men who served on the first day of the Somme battle. One feature of this wave of volunteers was the creation of the 'Pals' battalions formed from men who had a common background in communities, factories, sport clubs and businesses largely in the populous cities of northern England. Local politicians who had more enthusiasm than military experience raised a total of 134 battalions of the 'Pals'. The men who volunteered were better educated than most pre-war volunteers for the regular army, and motivated by the propaganda that had accompanied the outbreak of war against Germany and events such as the Zeppelin raids, which had caused British civilian casualties. Despite this enthusiasm, however, the vast majority of these volunteers knew nothing at all about soldiering in August 1914, while virtually every man over 20 on the continent had some military experience. It takes time and experience to turn civilians into soldiers, however well educated they are. Both time and experience were sadly lacking by the summer of 1916. To make matters worse, the majority of the 74,000 casualties suffered by the BEF in the early months of the war were the regulars and territorials who could have provided the experienced leadership the new soldiers needed. By January 1916 BEF casualties had reached over 510,000 and although the total force in France and Belgium now stood at over half a million men, too many of them were novice soldiers.

French

The pre-war French army was slightly smaller than the German (just under 4 million at the outbreak of war), a consequence of the falling birth rate. However, the men and those on the home front were keen to avenge the humiliating defeats of the Franco-Prussian War and to recover Alsace and Lorraine, which had been absorbed by the German Reich, and would demonstrate immense powers of endurance. The French army was old-fashioned even if its weapons were highly effective. Over-reliance on the bayonet was one cause of the heavy casualties suffered in the opening Battle of the Borders. This led to rapid changes, including camouflaged uniforms and tactical reform. The Battle of Verdun from February 1916 became a matter of pouring in reinforcements and suffering the consequences of attack and counter-attack. However, tactical lessons were learned and turned the French into a much more effective fighting force. By the outbreak of the Battle of the Somme, they were clearly superior to many of the British and it would be to the French that British generals looked for new methods of attack and defence during the course of the campaign. The French army learned that the weight of artillery was vital to success. As a result, unlike the BEF, the French army had a high concentration of artillery pieces of all calibres, including an abundance of heavy howitzers, guns and mortars capable of destroying German dugouts, cutting barbed wire and killing the German garrisons. It is no coincidence that the commander of the French 6th Army that attacked on the right flank of Rawlinson's 4th Army was General Marie Émile Fayolle, a gunner. His artillery force comprised 117 heavy batteries, including sixteen 8.6in howitzers and twenty-four 4.7in guns. The combined weight of fire was to overwhelm German defences and assist the infantry to break through the surviving defenders.

Critically, by the spring of 1916, few French units had not experienced the realities of trench warfare in both attack and defence. Joffre organised a rapid rotation of units serving at Verdun, which meant that, although the Germans assumed that the French divisions removed from the line had been destroyed, they had in fact been removed to rest before being employed on other fronts. On the Somme, these soldiers included reservists from Brittany and Normandy. South of the Somme, some of the men were colonial troops from North Africa, including Algerians and Senegalese. All were to demonstrate both 'dash' and a level of tactical sophistication that was to prove extremely effective on 1 July.

German

Motivation for German soldiers was provided by the common belief that their nation was the victim of an international conspiracy to deny them their rightful place among the empires of Europe. A united Germany was created by the military victories of the Austro-Prussian War (1866) and Franco-Prussian War. In consequence, many Germans believed that military victories were beneficial for a nation and its economy: what Germany needed was resources, space and people to become the economic powerhouse of Europe. This view was not shared by many of Germany's agricultural community. Unlike the urban population, many in the countryside foresaw potential disaster in a European war. Nonetheless, the men went off to war and the majority hoped for a short campaign and easy victory. By 1916, these assumptions had proved illusory but the concept of the universal conspiracy, fear of foreign invasion, the essential justice of their cause and the glory of the Empire kept German soldiers and civilians in the fight. Many believed that success required little more than to hold out until either the Russians in the east or the Allies in the west collapsed. What mattered was the will to win. One advantage enjoyed by the German soldier was that pre-war organisation meant that the local or regional depot combined infantry, artillery and cavalry into brigades and divisions which trained together. The rapid mobilisation of this force was critical. As the Schlieffen

Unlike Britain, the armies of mainland Europe consisted of conscripts and most German men over 20 had received military training. (Author's collection)

Plan called for rapid victory in the west before the army was largely transferred to the east, the German railway system was planned for both military and economic purposes. One feature of this mobilisation was an effective doubling of the German establishment by means of calling up all reservists to form reserve divisions which mirrored their regular formations, though weaker in artillery. Although the Schlieffen Plan was halted on the Marne in September 1914, the 'Old Army' proved to be a tenacious opponent, skilled in attack and counter-attack. The Germans began the war equipped with many of the weapons required for trench warfare, including grenades, mortars and heavy artillery. Although the German army started the war with a tactical doctrine based on the grand offensive, the advantage of digging-in led to the adoption of one based on digging-in deep and building defences in depth. The comparative lack of activity on the Somme during 1915 and early 1916 was used to good effect and the chalk subsoil proved ideal for the mining of deep dugouts. Unlike their British opponents, German units tended to hold sectors of the line for considerable periods, alternating battalions between the frontline, reserve and resting. As a result, German divisions were familiar with the ground they held and when engaged in building defences realised that they, rather than a relieving formation, would receive the benefit of their hard work. Such was the pace of the building programme that some men complained life was easier in the frontline than when they were working on trench construction.

Weapons

The British infantryman of 1914 had gone to war armed with a Short Magazine Lee–Enfield (SMLE) rifle, ammunition and a bayonet. As a regular, reservist or territorial soldier he was well trained with the SMLE, for great reliance was put on both the infantry's rate of fire and its accuracy. Soldiers of the BEF were expected to fire at least fifteen rounds per minute and to be able to hit targets up to the maximum sighted range of 2,000yd. Every battalion of roughly 1,000 men had the support of two Maxim or Vickers machine guns capable of firing up to 600 rounds per minute to the same range as rifles, normally up to 2,000yd. British artillery largely consisted of the 18lb field gun, which was in many respects similar in range and rate of fire to the French 75mm (2.95in) and German 77mm (3.03in) guns. These weapons were effective up to about 6,000–8,000yd and could fire at least fifteen shells per minute.

The difference was that the BEF lacked the large number of medium and heavy guns that its ally and enemy could deploy. The BEF was conceived as a mobile force intended for manoeuvre warfare in the open. Although the infantry and artillery performed well in the opening actions, while outgunned by German artillery, the conditions of trench warfare meant that virtually every aspect of weaponry and training had to be reconsidered. The infantry were issued with the Lewis 'automatic rifle', which could supplement the volume of fire. This weapon was air-cooled and much lighter than the water-cooled Vickers. By the end of 1915, these weapons were removed from the infantry battalions and used en masse as part of the newly created Machine Gun Corps. Further innovation followed in the form of grenades or 'bombs' as they were known by the British army. Grenades had been available to German troops, for use in attacking fortresses, since the start of the war, but not to the BEF. Initially, British bombs were improvised from tins and locally available explosives, some provided by the French. By 1915, these were being manufactured in large numbers in the United Kingdom, the most famous being the Mills pattern. Specialist bombers in the infantry would in time be able to fire them at great range using their rifles. These rifle bombs were in common use by late 1915 and were useful in trench-to-trench action although quite how they were to be used in the attack was not fully resolved. Mortars were larger and had greater range. These were unknown to the British in 1914; the first patterns were manufactured in workshops just behind the lines by the Indian Corps and then other units. These were at first a stop-gap, but proved the basis for an excellent weapon in the form of Mr Stokes' 'intelligent drain pipe'. Whilst heavy mortars were the province of the artillery and were fired by gunners, by 1916 infantry battalions had their own mortar batteries, providing the advantage of high-angle plunging fire.

The artillery of the BEF went into action in 1914 in many cases firing over 'open sights' at targets that the gunners could see. The consequence of this was heavy losses of both guns and gunners, and within weeks of the outbreak of war guns were being fired directed by forward observation officers and later by the aircraft of the Royal Flying Corps. Medium and heavy guns, specifically howitzers, which could lob shells high into the air to destroy trenches and dugouts, were in immediate demand and their manufacture began in earnest in 1915. Sadly, industry could not provide sufficient guns or ammunition. In the resulting 'shell scandal' of early 1915 gunners were told to ration shells and were unable to respond to German fire or properly support the infantry. One consequence of this was the central organisation of production by the Minister for Munitions, Lloyd George, whose prime ministership was largely won by his ability to resolve the shell shortage by the spring of 1916. Sadly, although shells were available they were largely for the light field guns and manufacturing mistakes made in factories with no background in munitions resulted in up to one-third not functioning as intended. Dud shells and premature explosions, which damaged guns and killed and wounded their crews, were a feature of the British experience of the Somme.

A key task in preparing for the 'Big Push' was the destruction of German barbed wire and other defences. This required large numbers of big guns. There were too few weapons like this 8in Howitzer. (IWM Q569)

On the outbreak of war the commanders intended to use shrapnel rather than high explosives. Shrapnel shells were fused to burst in the air above enemy troops in the open. Each shell contained hundreds of metallic balls that could inflict devastating casualties on troops in the open. Once trenches were established, shrapnel shells were less effective than high explosives that detonated on contact with the ground. Sadly, manufacturers were simply unable to produce enough high explosives. The preliminary bombardment fired by the guns of the BEF thus consisted, largely, of shrapnel shells that were ineffective. Shrapnel could cut barbed wire providing the shell was fused to burst close to the ground and release a dense cloud of balls to hit the wire at maximum velocity. Sadly for the infantry many gunners were, like the rest of the army, under-trained, and they would not fully master the accurate fusing and directing of shells until 1917. More sensitive fuses that went off on first contact with barbed wire or the ground, increasing their effect and reducing cratering, would not be available in significant numbers until late in the battle. One other result of this lack of skill was the simple fact that most British gunners were incapable of providing a barrage of shells like their French allies. The barrage was intended to provide a curtain or line of shells that could be controlled in such a way as to move ahead of the advancing 'friendly' infantry. If this was done well the barrage would advance ahead of an infantry attack and the men could use the shells as both a form of cover against enemy fire and also to force enemy defenders to take cover. In theory the attackers could reach their opponents' trenches before the latter could man the parapet and effectively open fire. In the early fighting the British bombardment often simply ceased as the infantry closed on the enemy position, leaving the Germans time to man their trenches.

Notable on the opening day of the Somme offensive was the BEF's extensive use of mines and tunnels. One of the most visited locations on the Western Front is the site of Lochnagar Crater, close to La Boisselle; and tens of thousands of tourists stare into this vast hole every year. This crater 450ft in diameter, its rim about 15ft above the surface, was created by two charges laid in chambers 50ft below the surface. The total charge was 60,000lb of ammonal. Few realise that the Lochnagar mine was one of two blown simultaneously either side of the village, the other was called 'Y Sap', or that nineteen

A vital task given to the artillery in the preliminary bombardment before the battle was cutting the barbed wire. This image shows that it was possible to cut wire, but that it could create alternative obstacles to the advance. (IWM Q832)

other mines were used that morning. Two others failed to detonate. For months before the battle, five Royal Engineer Tunnelling Companies had worked to create an elaborate chain of mines and saps. The 40,000lb Hawthorn Redoubt mine at Beaumont-Hamel was blown at 7.20 a.m., the rest at or close to 7.28 a.m. This allowed the debris to fall to earth before the attackers moved into the area of the explosion. Some mines at the end of shallow tunnels that emerged close to the German frontline allowed troops to cross no-man's-land in relative safely. One mine to the south of La Boisselle featured a vast offensive flamethrower intended to incinerate the enemy garrison at zero hour. The tunnels into no-man's-land, such as that which allowed two companies of 1st Lancashire Fusiliers to reach the protection of the sunken lane in front of Beaumont-Hamel, indicate the complexity of planning that went into the Somme offensive.

Geoffrey Malins filmed the explosion of the Hawthorn mine and described it:

The ground where I stood gave a mighty convulsion. It rocked and swayed. I gripped hold of my tripod to steady myself. Then for all the world like a gigantic sponge, the earth rose high in the air to the height of hundreds of feet. Higher and higher it rose, and with a horrible grinding roar the earth settles back upon itself, leaving in its place a mountain of smoke.

Tactics

In popular imagination, the infantrymen simply waited for the whistles before scaling ladders onto the parapet on the first day of the Somme. From here, they advanced with rifle and bayonet at a walking pace across no-man's-land towards an alert and well-armed enemy to be mown down by German machine gun fire. Countless films and television programmes have reinforced this, as did the two brief pieces of film made by the official cameraman, Geoffrey Malins, showing precisely this form of attack. It is now known that Malins filmed these sequences at the Trench Mortar School near Saint-Pol, which is not even on the Somme. No one died in this filming and the men involved 'play acted' for the camera. This does not mean that this simple tactic was not used, only that it was one of many used in the attack of 1 July. General Rawlinson left it to individual commanders to decide the best tactics for the terrain they were in, the nature of the enemy defences and the level of training the troops had achieved. At least a third of the attackers on 1 July advanced at a run, frequently in 'Indian file' one behind another so they could exploit gaps in defences and provide a limited target to defenders. Elsewhere, attackers crawled out into no-man's-land using specially prepared saps, underground Russian saps (shallow tunnels) or simply the cover of long grass and vegetation. The remainder largely advanced at a walk and with rifles at high port, confident that the bombardment of the previous week had done its work. Some unit commanders confidently assured their troops that 'not even a rat' could have survived the shelling. Advancing in the line meant that the men would arrive at the enemy position at the same time and could deal with any pockets of resistance collectively. This confidence would prove misplaced, but it must be remembered that the week of shelling 'looked' effective, despite a few reports to the contrary.

If British commanders placed too much reliance on the capacity of the artillery to destroy German defences, kill the defenders and cut the barbed wire, they also realised how potentially vulnerable the infantry would be if counter-attacked without the support of the guns. They realised that the poorly trained infantry might simply advance too far and too fast. The problem was that the field guns had to be placed behind the British frontline and concealed from observation. Most were at least 2,000yd behind the most advanced British positions. With their maximum range of roughly 6,000yd, they could only hit targets within 4,000yd of the British trenches. Once British troops crossed no-man's-land and advanced into the enemy position the artillery's targets would quickly exceed their maximum range. It was thus decided that the attackers could not simply keep on going after a successful attack, even if there were no defenders to face. The infantry would have to halt and dig-in to wait until first the field guns and then the rest of the artillery was brought forward, if not into the captured area then at least close to the old frontline. This was far from easy as the majority of the guns were drawn by horses and the area across which these guns, limbers and ammunition wagons were to advance was criss-crossed with trenches, barbed wire and shell holes. Technology restricted the exploitation of success and even cavalry, should it be sent forward following a breakthrough, would face the same problems of movement in the devastated zone as it advanced. When tanks were deployed on the battlefield in mid-September their caterpillar tracks and armoured sides were able to deal with some of the obstacles, but the craters and trenches remained a major problem. The motto of the tank corps became 'Through the Mud and the Blood to the Green Fields Beyond' reflecting the promise that a real breakthrough offered.

Uniform, Equipment and Kit

It is arguable that the British soldier in the Battle of the Somme was the best clothed and equipped. His SMLE rifle carried a magazine of ten rounds, more than any other soldier on the field. His offensive Mills bombs were highly effective and reliable. Although not smart, the khaki wool uniform was warm and serviceable, offering roomy

British troops were rehearsing their attacks throughout the preliminary bombardment. Here 4th Worcesters of 29th Division leave the training area at Acheux in high spirits. (IWM Q740)

pockets. The 1908 Web Equipment supplied to most regulars and territorials was far superior to any other equipment set, being a similar colour to the uniform, well balanced and providing the user access to up to 150 rounds of rifle ammunition. The pattern 1914 leather equipment issued to the men of the New Armies was not quite as good as the Mills pattern, but was equal to those used by French or German troops. Like the French, every frontline soldier in the BEF was issued with a steel helmet, a piece of equipment the German troops would not enjoy until September 1916. The PH helmet could filter out most gases and was replaced by the much better Small Box Respirator in September. This pattern was the best available and would remain in use until the outbreak of the Second World War twenty-three years later.

BEST INFANTRY EQUIPMENT AVAILABLE

At a pre-war demonstration of the 1908 Web Equipment, the inventor put on a fully loaded set of the webbing and walked across the room on his hands to demonstrate how well balanced it was.

One of the many problems surrounding the events of 1 July remains the amount of kit each British soldier carried into action. Some have suggested that the weight was excessive. John Keegan describes the British attack on the Somme: 'The manoeuvre was to be done slowly and deliberately, for the men were to be laden with about sixty pounds of equipment, their re-supply with food and ammunition during the battle being one of the things the staff could not guarantee.' A few writers have gone so far as to suggest that the load contributed to failure when the men went 'over the top'. A.J.P. Taylor suggests that

> On 1 July, thirteen British divisions went forward together. The men threaded their way through the British wire; then formed into a solid line, and sought to advance. Though their one chance was speed, they were weighed down by 66 lb. of equipment, and often much more – field telephones, carrier pigeons, picks and shovels.

Taylor appears to be quoting the figure given by Sir James Edmonds, the official historian of the British army, who further stated that this load 'made it difficult to get out of a trench, impossible to move much quicker than a slow walk, or to rise and lie down quickly'. This argument was seized upon by the famous military historian Basil Liddell Hart, who described the Somme as a 'race' to the German trenches. A race the British lost by three minutes, mown down as they struggled through no-mans-land under their excessive loads. The real footage shot on 1 July from Beaumont-Hamel, and still images taken elsewhere, shows men running forward despite the very load described as 'weighing them down' and making it 'impossible' to do so. If we dismiss the idea of it being impossible to carry the weight, we might consider first what the load consisted of and then why it was felt necessary to give the infantrymen such a burden.

For a soldier to be effective he must be armed and have some means of personal defence. On 1 July 1916 this meant for most infantrymen a rifle and bayonet, sufficient ammunition to use in the event of a protracted battle, plus at least two grenades. He needed a helmet and a respirator in case of gas attack. Certain specialists, such as Lewis Gunners, bombers and signallers, had their loads adjusted to reflect their role. However, every man going into action required drinking water, rations and the means to prepare them, some form of waterproof and items required for health and hygiene. A few items, such as his paybook and identification tag, were intended to identify his body if the worst happened. On a more optimistic note, soldiers carried field dressing to deal with wounds. Although one way of avoiding wounds was to kill the enemy, a more certain way of achieving some level of safety was to provide a means of digging-in. Troops thus carried pickaxes and shovels besides the standard issue entrenching tools. If an enemy position was captured the trenches would need to be reversed, so troops also carried sandbags for reveting and flares and rockets to indicate the newly established trenches to the artillery observers and Royal Flying Corps.

Communication was vital for success and in addition to wireless and telephones carrier pigeons were employed in large numbers. Here a basket of pigeons is carried to the front while the mobile pigeon loft awaits their return with messages. (IWM CO2171)

It was anticipated that most troops would be replaced in the line by new units within twenty-four hours. As this could not be assured, many units carried extra water, ammunition, food and basic supplies. Elsewhere, specialist units were detailed to act as 'carriers' to slowly follow up the advance with an even heavier burden than the attack waves. By the summer of 1916, no infantry commander wished to face the inevitable German counter-attack with his men handicapped by shortages, possibly for days, before relief. Few men, therefore, went into action on 1 July with a load weighing less than 70lb. The events of that day demonstrated that little of this load could have been left behind.

THE DAYS BEFORE BATTLE

Preparations for the Somme

In early 1916 the German defensive system on the Somme was based on two prepared lines with a third ready for construction. The two lines were 2,000–4,000yd apart and the forward defensive system was fixed on a series of defended villages interspersed with supporting redoubts and strongpoints. It was calculated that if the British first line fell, an assault on the second line would involve them in a time consuming redeployment of their light and medium artillery. The villages, though largely ruined, were prepared for defence and featured mined shelters under the buildings, command posts, extensive belts of barbed wire, trenches and machine gun positions. The great advantage of ruined buildings was that the rubble detonated shells before they penetrated beneath. Standing structures did not provide this cushioning effect. The second line shared many features of the first and had the added advantage of being largely on a reverse slope, out of direct observation. A particularly important component of the defensive system was the web of deep buried telephone cables supplemented, in the event of their being cut, by artillery fire, by lamps, horns, pigeons and well-trained teams of runners as backup.

MAXIM'S MACHINE GUN

The machine guns used by both the German army and the BEF were based on a design by Hiram Maxim, who was born in the United States although he became a British citizen in 1900. Ironically, he died in 1916 without ever fully knowing the effect of his weapon on the battlefields of the Great War.

Each defensive line comprised three or more lines of trenches providing mutual support and accommodation. This accommodation was built to resist the penetrating power of the heavy artillery and German troops generally had the benefit of deeply excavated dugouts. Work on the deepest dugouts had not begun until the spring of 1916 and, although some shelters were at least 30ft (10m) deep with multiple entrances, some interconnected by tunnels, there was still work to be completed in some areas. Abundant barbed wire had been placed in belts and full use was made of natural features such as Y Ravine at Beaumont-Hamel, which provided natural cover for the defenders. Redoubts largely capable of all round defence were created. In many areas, German frontline positions also had the benefit of high ground to the rear. This meant that machine guns and also artillery observers could see both no-man's-land and the area likely to be occupied if an Allied attack was initially successful. The result was a system of defence stronger than anything seen before, and which was most fully developed north of Fricourt. To the south, the ground was not so advantageous to the defenders. In this area, the German defences lacked suitable observation positions and the rear and frontline positions tended to be closer together. One element of German tactical doctrine that favoured the Allies was immediate counter-attack to prevent ground being lost. This meant that in many areas frontline positions were relatively heavily held by German troops. This favoured the attackers as it concentrated troops in the area under the most intense bombardment, resulting in heavier casualties than was necessary. The German defenders had to be able to survive any preliminary bombardment and still be capable of

By early 1916 the German army had dug-in well-defended positions like this one on the Somme. (Author's collection)

manning their trenches before the attackers could cross no-man's-land and enter the trench system.

However, even if this happened the machine guns with direct observation could engage the attackers from their rear positions and the artillery could open fire under orders from forward observation officers or simply fire onto prearranged positions either on their own trenches or as a curtain in no-man's-land. This would cut off initially successful attacking troops from reinforcement and resupply. The Germans rehearsed these procedures intensively in the months before the battle.

The British Army's Plan of Attack

When 4th Army was established in January 1916 its commander was Sir Henry Rawlinson. He spent his first few weeks of command carrying out a study of the Ypres Salient as a suitable position for an offensive later in the year. As the Allied plan changed, 4th Army was moved to the Somme, taking over the sector from the River Somme to Fonquevillers. In early March Haig gave Rawlinson the task of

Key features of the German defensive system were the use of deep dugouts and barbed wire. (IWM Q890)

planning an offensive in conjunction with French forces operating to the south of the Somme. Initially, Rawlinson was given the overall objective of using artillery to overwhelm the Germans' first- and second-line defences on a frontage from Maricourt to Serre, before using the infantry to achieve a breakthrough. This was to be followed by exploitation of the breach by reserves, including cavalry. Following Verdun priorities changed, and the plan adapted, but there was soon conflict between Haig's ambitious policy of a broad front and deep penetration, and Rawlinson's more cautious step-by-step 'bite and hold' approach.

'Bite and Hold'

Rawlinson based his policy on a number of factors, all of which were interrelated. The first was the relationship between the size of force available and the number of heavy guns that could be deployed. The five army corps in 4th Army dictated a front of approximately 20,000yd with eight or nine men per yard and 200 guns of 6in calibre or above providing coverage of one gun per 100yd. The range of these guns and the more numerous field batteries next dictated the depth of each phase of advance. The heavy guns could cut wire and destroy defences at ranges up to 4–5,000yd; beyond that there were problems of accuracy and observation. As a result, Rawlinson advocated initially breaching the first line and then reorganising over a period of about three days and moving the guns forward before attempting to attack the German second-line positions. This, he argued, had the advantage of drawing German reinforcements into the 'killing ground' for they were bound to counter-attack. Critically, it meant that the British infantry would operate under cover of their artillery support, and that this support would compensate for their variable quality, especially if they became disorganised, which was likely, or faced counter-attack, which was certain. The plan also dictated that no British infantry would have to advance more than 3,000yd in a single attack. This approach simplified the battle but slowed the pace of breakthrough; it met with the approval of Rawlinson's corps commanders. Rawlinson also advocated a lengthy preliminary bombardment lasting not less than fifty to sixty hours (spanning four to five days). This would provide time to cut the enemy wire and potentially destroy many of the German defences, as it would allow the artillery to observe the effect of their fire and make the necessary adjustments. Unlike at Loos, large-scale use of gas did not feature in the plan, although smoke cover was advocated, as was mining to destroy major German strongpoints.

FROM NOVELTY TO WEAPON SYSTEM

The first heavier-than-air craft to fly across the English Channel was piloted by Louis Blériot in 1909. The Royal Flying Corps was established as a branch of the British army in 1912. Two years later, on the outbreak of war, the first RFC aircraft flew across the channel and was being used for reconnaissance within weeks. By 1915 aircraft were carrying weapons and being used to direct artillery and take aerial photographs. Four years later, an aircraft piloted by Alcock and Brown flew across the Atlantic Ocean.

In addition to twenty-one mines of various sizes, surprises for the German defenders included the use of a British flamethrower near Fricourt. Here is a British flamethrower demonstrated in training. (IWM Q14938)

The Ambitious Alternative

General Haig rejected Rawlinson's plan as too cautious and lacking any element of surprise. It also failed to take into account the changed role of the French forces that were now to attack in corps strength on the northern bank of the Somme. In light of these criticisms, Rawlinson was forced to redraft his plans and resubmit them to GHQ in mid-April. In this new plan, provision was made to seize objectives in the German second line, although this would have the effect of dispersing the artillery support and would certainly increase the risks involved. Rawlinson, however, refused to reduce the length of the preliminary bombardment, arguing that he could not produce a 'hurricane' bombardment in the few hours that Haig had advocated with a fixed number of guns. One major deception plan was made and in late April VII Corps of Allenby's 3rd Army was given the task of mounting a diversionary attack against the heavily defended Gommecourt Salient to the north of 4th Army's assault. This attack was not to be exploited; its purpose was to divert artillery fire and reinforcements from the offensive further south. To draw increased German attention to this area, preparations were made as obvious as possible in the hope of deceiving them as to the frontage and direction of the forthcoming assault. For the same reason, wire cutting was carried out on the fronts of both 1st and 2nd Armies.

Final response from GHQ took until mid-May, by which time aerial reconnaissance had discovered that the Germans were building a third defensive line, which made 4th Army's task still more difficult. Despite this development, it was clear Haig still thought the German defences could be made to collapse. He continued to pressure Rawlinson to plan for an even more ambitious alternative in which the cavalry reserve and Gough's Reserve Army might be pushed through the breach created by 4th Army, especially if the high ground on the dominant spurs at Miramont and around Pozières were captured. It was hoped that this force would break out towards Arras and roll up the German defences from south to north. The plan that eventually evolved was a series of compromises that fully suited neither those planning nor conducting the operations. It was driven by major political considerations and the requirement to co-operate, as a junior partner, with a demanding ally. The plan was ultimately based on the belief that the artillery could do sufficient damage to the German defences to get the infantry across no-man's-land and into the enemy position before the Germans could respond.

CATTLE RANCH TO BATTLEFIELD

Barbed wire was patented in the United States in 1867, two years after the American Civil War ended. The military potential for this method of controlling cattle was soon recognised by the armies of the world and it was used extensively in the Boer War and the Russo-Japanese War. Today, barbed wire is a symbol of the Great War and strands of wire laid on the Western Front between 1914 and 1918 can still be found.

On the matter of timing, it was decided in consultation with the French that the British and French north of the Somme would attack at 7.30 a.m., well after dawn, and half an hour later than Rawlinson had requested. This timing, it was argued, would facilitate observation of the advance and allow for maximum use of Allied artillery to deal with German strongpoints or counter-attacks. The attack would thus be made in full daylight, as had the British attack at Loos and the German assault at Verdun. By the time this decision had been reached Rawlinson had abandoned his initial plan to use smoke to assist the entire attack and ultimately left corps commanders to decide whether to employ smoke or not. There was little synchronisation of timing, methods of attack, use of mines and even jumping off positions. Despite the common image of lines of infantry leaving their trenches with fixed bayonets to walk towards the German lines, this tactic was rarely used on 1 July. Some battalions attempted to rush no-man's-land; others advanced at a slow walk. Some units advanced in waves; others in columns, platoons advancing in single file. Some battalions made their way into specially dug assembly trenches either in no-man's-land or immediately behind the British lines. In a few cases the infantry avoided signalling their intentions and simply filed out into no-man's-land before dawn to wait for 7.30 a.m. and the signal to attack.

Preparing for Z Day – Artillery, Barbed Wire and Dugouts

Each of the five days of the British artillery preparation was given a code letter, beginning with U and ending on Y Day. U Day, the first of the preliminary bombardment, was fixed for 24 June, which meant that Z Day, the attack, was initially planned for 29 June. On paper, the artillery force assembled for the bombardment looked formidable: over 1,400 British guns of all calibres available to fire more than 1.6 million shells at the German defences. In addition, the French were supporting their own assault and providing extra weight to the British bombardment in the southern sector. This unprecedented bombardment had three objectives. The first was to cut the German wire in front of their first- and second-line defences. This task was

For an assault to be effective, artillery fire needed to be observed, a task that was carried out by the Royal Flying Corps. In bad weather, aircraft such as the DH2 could not fly. This failure delayed the offensive by two days. (IWM Q67534)

largely given to the more than 1,000 field guns, which used more than 1 million shrapnel shells to this end. In some areas, specifically in the northern front, heavy guns were diverted from other tasks to assist with wire cutting, thus depriving other areas of their weight of fire. The second objective, which was left to the 283 howitzers of 6in calibre and above, was the destruction of the trenches and dugouts of the German defensive system, and the death or neutralisation of their occupants. A total of 188,500 weapons were used here. The final task was the destruction of defending artillery by means of counter-battery fire, which was largely left to the 160 heavy guns not used on other engagements. At this stage in the war methods of locating hidden guns other than by direct observation were basic and it was unlikely that the German artillery would be overwhelmed.

Early in the bombardment bad weather in the form of mist, low cloud and rain hampered British observation. Balloons and the observation aircraft of the RFC were grounded and even observation officers on the ground were unable to adjust fire or assess the effect of the shooting. As a result, on 28 June Rawlinson postponed the assault for two days to improve the artillery's chances of carrying out its tasks. This decision increased the number of shells fired overall, but reduced the numbers available for the guns on 1 July. When firing was possible, problems were experienced with fuses; some heavy shells exploded prematurely and others failed to function at all. This was compounded by bad fuse setting for the 18lb field guns that were meant to breach the wire. Detonated too high, these lacked the energy to cut the thick German wire; too low and the shells either cut small sections to pieces or exploded on contact with the ground.

The Other Side of the Hill – What was the Effect?

The bombardment produced patchy results and, despite raids and patrols being mounted during periodic lulls in the bombardment, information was partial and ambiguous. On the front of XIII Corps patrols noted the wire well cut and XV Corps reported that the only area in which the wire was not destroyed was that facing 21st Division. Further north the news was not so good: VIII Corps noted that the wire had been cut in some places in front of 29th Division, but much less so opposite 4th and 31st Divisions. To some extent, raids during nocturnal lulls in the bombardment provided similarly varied results.

British shells falling on German trenches. On the left, a large-calibre high-explosive shell has detonated. Note the number of shrapnel shells, indicated by small smoke clouds, detonating to the right. (IWM Q23)

In the southern sector a few prisoners were taken, some of whom reported that the dugouts had been destroyed whilst others stated that they were largely undamaged. The lack of successful raids in the northern sector led to the erroneous conclusion that the results of the bombardment were broadly uniform, though generally more successful further south. Unfortunately, one reason that the British raids were unsuccessful was the robust German response. Despite the days spent shelling enemy artillery, barrages were reported as variously 'heavy', 'active' and 'moderate'. Post-war reports indicated that few German guns had been destroyed, many more had arrived to reinforce the defences, and over 590 field and 240 heavy guns, many undetected, now awaited the assault. The wire uncut in some sectors and German artillery still in action, it is now clear that success on Z Day was by no means certain. Among the commanders on the ground uncertain of the real situation on the enemy side of no-man's-land, and aware that the attack could not be cancelled, a feeling of cautious optimism prevailed.

The artillery plan called for a peak level of bombardment to be reached from 7 a.m. and then for the guns to gradually increase the range as the infantry advanced. This fixed timetable was rigid in some areas and called for a series of lifts in which the shelling would cease in one area and then start further into the enemy position. On the front of XIII, XV and VIII Corps a different approach was tried: a creeping barrage in which a curtain of shells was advanced across the battlefield ahead of the infantry. This sophisticated technique would become standard by 1917, but it was an innovation on the Somme.

Military Intelligence

For the Germans the question remained: when would the assault be launched? In some areas units found it impossible to get food or water or to relieve men in frontline positions. In some cases dugouts collapsed under the bombardment and the battlefield looked like a moonscape. If the men of 4th Army felt that Z Day would be a surprise to the Germans, they were to be bitterly disappointed. German observers had already calculated that the fourteen balloons they could count indicated fourteen divisions and that the intensity of the

Mametz under bombardment. Note the destruction in the area under attack compared with inside Allied lines. The artillery preparation 'looked' to be very effective. (IWM Q114)

bombardment further indicated where the blow would fall. However, the actual date remained a problem. Some information came from agents and still more from aerial reconnaissance, as the build-up of guns and stores indicated that the offensive was pending. However, a message from XIV Reserve Corps on 26 June, after the preliminary bombardment had commenced, indicated that the main attack would be on 27 June. This information came from a wounded British prisoner who was left behind in no-man's-land under fire. The prisoner also offered additional detail, indicating that the attack would take place on a 30-mile front from Gommecourt to the south. He even stated that the bombardment would last four or five days. A few days later prisoners from a disastrous raid by 29th Division and a deserter from the same division provided more detail and confirmation of the date.

FAULTY FUSES

One problem encountered by British artillery was the unreliability of fuses fitted to high-explosive shells. These tended to function well after impact, creating craters as they exploded after they penetrated deep into the ground. The craters acted as obstacles, especially if they flooded, but also provided protection for troops.

The information about the timing of the attack was useless as the two-day extension to the artillery programme meant that Z Day had been moved. However, this final detail was provided by German listening stations, which were able to hear British telephone messages that were often not in code, up to 3,000yd away. As a result, in the early hours of 1 July an intercept of a message from 34th Division made it clear that the offensive was imminent.

The French Sector

General Joffre had initially planned for the battle on the Somme to be part of a larger campaign whose objective was to push German forces back by means of a battle of attrition. Once Falkenhayn seized the initiative by attacking Verdun plans for the Somme were gradually scaled down so that a single French army would attack on 1 July. Ultimately, Joffre was able to commit fewer men to the initial phase of the battle than the British. Initially the plan proposed by General Foch had been to wait a matter of days after the British assault before mounting his own attack, but under pressure from Haig this plan was abandoned. As an alternative, one corps of the French 6th Army, General Fayolle's, was placed north of the Somme to protect the flank of the remaining two corps that were to operate on the southern bank of the river. North of the Somme Fayolle deployed XX 'Iron' Corps, which had an impressive battlefield reputation. This corps was to attack at the same time as the British, 7.30 a.m. South of the river the I Colonial Corps on the left and XXXV Corps on the right were to wait two more hours before making their own independent attack.

The French army was well equipped with heavy weapons such as this railway gun. Effective artillery preparation in the French sector of the offensive greatly improved the success of their attack. (IWM Q70524)

A fourth corps, II Corps, was kept in reserve. No preparation by the French on the Somme, specifically the preliminary artillery bombardment, could go unnoticed by the Germans. However, their own intelligence had suggested that the French, worn down by Verdun, were incapable of mounting an attack. The preparations were interpreted as a feint and not a threat. Ironically, if intelligence failings by the British meant that surprise was not to be achieved by the BEF, it was the failure of German high command to foresee the potential for a French attack astride the Somme that helped their Allies' great success.

THE BATTLEFIELD:
WHAT ACTUALLY HAPPENED?

The First Day

	04.00–06.25	German batteries bombard the British frontline at Gommecourt
	06.25	Hurricane bombardment commences on German positions
	07.00	Mist in area of Carnoy lifts
	07.15–07.22	Entrances to Russian saps in no-man's-land are blown
1 July 1916	07.20	Mine is blown under Hawthorn Redoubt at Beaumont-Hamel
	07.27–07.28	Remaining large mines are blown
	07.30	The main assault begins on the Somme
	08.30	Elements of 36th Division are 1 mile behind German lines
	08.45	63rd Brigade of 21st Division reaches its objective at La Boisselle
	09.00	The Newfoundland Regiment is cut down behind British lines while trying to reach its objective
		Elements of 8th Division attempt attack on German second-line positions at Ovillers

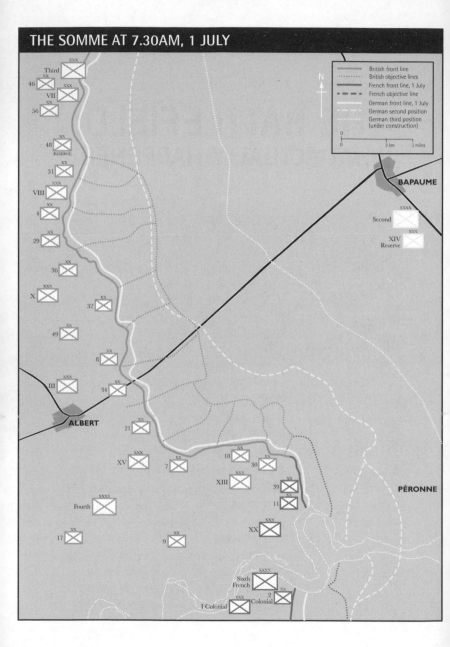

THE SOMME AT 7.30AM, 1 JULY

British front line
British objective lines
French front line, 1 July
French objective line
German front line, 1 July
German second position
German third position (under construction)

0   2 km
0   2 miles

N

BAPAUME

Third

46
VII
56

48
RESERVE

31
VIII
4

29

36
X
32

49

8

III
34

21
ALBERT

XV   7
18   30
XIII
39
11

XX

17   9

Second

XIV
Reserve

PÉRONNE

Fourth

Sixth
French   2
I Colonial Colonial

	09.15	An observer reports men of 31st Division are in the village of Serre
	09.30	French attack south of the Somme
		56th Division reaches most of its objectives at Gommecourt
	10.30	Remains of 16th Middlesex and 2nd Royal Fusiliers retreat from the crater at Beaumont-Hamel
	11.00	Village of Montauban is captured
		Signal seen from German second line at Gommecourt indicating progress of 46th Division
1 July 1916	12.30	French 39th Division reaches its final objectives
	12.34	British 30th Division capture La Briqueterie command post
	14.00	7th Division outflank the village of Mametz
	16.00	Mametz cleared of enemy by 7th Division
		18th and 30th Divisions consolidating their final positions
	19.30	VIII Corps have been driven out of most of the positions captured earlier in the day
	21.30	Final men from 46th Division return to British lines from no-man's-land at Gommecourt
	21.50	Plan to attack with remains of 31st Division is cancelled
	22.30	Most of 36th Division are driven back to the British frontline by German counter-attacks

To make the operations of 1 July easier to understand, I have organised this chapter into a series of separate sections each dealing with a corps sector and its objectives. These sections run from south to north. My reason for doing this is to challenge the belief that the first day of the Somme was a disaster. This is largely true of the area north of the Albert–Bapaume road, but even here there were local successes. As a counterpoint to the tragedy that unfolded on the northern flank, however, the southern attack was a triumph.

2 MILLION MEN IN ARMS

The strength of the BEF in November 1916 was 2,054,277.

The French Sector

South of the River Somme two French corps, I Colonial and XXXV, advanced at 9.30 a.m., two hours later than their comrades in XX Corps on the bank. They discovered that the eight-day bombardment had been more effective in this area than any other part of the Allied front. The German artillery had been virtually silenced and the focus of the German defence was isolated machine gun positions and small groups of infantrymen. The advance was not hurried and the experienced French *poilus* took advantage of every crater and fold in the ground to conceal their movements. Their tactics used a combination of light automatic weapons to provide supporting fire while small groups of infantry infiltrated weak spots in the defences to cut off defenders and overwhelm strongpoints. They systematically cleared the Germans from their pulverised defences and rounded up hundreds of demoralised prisoners. Although the well-defended village of Frise proved a difficult objective, by the end of the advance the French had reached the German second-line positions and taken over 3,000 prisoners. The day was a clear triumph for the French. It appeared that the road to Péronne and beyond was open and that a renewed advance would follow the next morning.

XX Corps

The French troops north of the River Somme went into attack at 7.30 a.m., at the same time as their British Allies. By the time they left their trenches, conditions for the German troops had become a nightmare. General Bafourier's Corps attacked an enemy whose barbed wire entanglements had been largely destroyed by heavy French artillery fire. German trenches had collapsed and shells had penetrated even some of the deepest dugouts. The surviving members of the German garrison had abandoned their shattered positions and were dispersed in shell craters. Only a gallant few of the defenders were capable of putting up resistance as the French infantry advanced. By 12.30 p.m., the men of the French 39th Division had reached their final objectives without having to call upon any of their reserves. In some cases, French troops had advanced a further half-mile beyond their objective. They found little sign of the enemy and there appeared to be a real opportunity to exploit the disarray in the German defences. By about 1.30 p.m. General Bafourier was in contact with his British counterpart from XIII Corps urging him to continue the advance. He was aware that for the French to proceed without flanking protection from the British on their left would invite disaster should the Germans counter-attack. The response he received did not help Anglo-French relations. General Congreve declined on the basis that Rawlinson had stressed the importance of securing the positions captured and preparing for the next step in the advance. Importantly, on his left 18th Division had not cleared its objectives and XV Corps was not fully successful, potentially exposing his left flank. Despite further calls to advance, both the British and French corps held the ground they had reached by the end of the day. The British 18th and French 39th Divisions fought off half-hearted counter-attacks during the latter part of the afternoon and evening.

British 4th Army

XIII Corps – Montauban

By comparison with other sectors of the Somme front, the troops who attacked at Montauban had numerous factors in their favour. They were about to advance with the French XX Corps on their right flank and it was clear from early in the preliminary bombardment that the additional weight of fire provided by the French artillery had been highly effective. The German artillery in this area was badly handled and good aerial reconnaissance, which spotted the enemy guns, their number and calibre, meant that few German batteries were still in action on 1 July. Raids in the days preceding the attack had shown that the wire was well cut and German defences comprehensively wrecked. Only a few especially deep dugouts survived the bombardment and a projectile from a French heavy mortar destroyed the German headquarters in Glatz Redoubt. Worse still for the defenders, a relief of the garrison by recently arrived Bavarian units was in progress. As a result, when the assault was launched, many German soldiers were dazed, confused or simply lost.

The topography here did not provide the Germans with the good observation positions offered further north, and the trenches were close together to provide weight of fire, making a better target for artillery. Perhaps the most critical factor to ensure success was the standard of the troops in the two infantry divisions involved. The 18th Division was a Kitchener unit recruited from London and the South-East of England. It had as its commander Major General Ivor Maxse, a brilliant trainer of soldiers who had turned the unpromising raw material of 1914 into one of the best trained divisions in the BEF. Maxse was an innovator, but at the same time sceptical about the overemphasis, common in the BEF, on the employment of grenades. He trained his men to avoid being drawn into 'bombing' duels, which were often inconclusive, and instead to use the bayonet and small arms to advance, if necessary getting behind opponents and outflanking their positions.

The corps commander, Major General R. Wanless O'Gowan, decided to employ one of the first British creeping barrages. This curtain of shells falling at a distance ahead of the attacking troops prevented the enemy garrison from firing until the British were close to their trenches. A final rush onto the defences by the attackers usually found the German soldiers either still in the remaining dugouts or very willing to surrender. The reason for this can be found in this German description of conditions close to Carnoy: 'two thirds of the dugout entrances were buried in most areas by the plum pudding mines [2in mortar bombs] and became unusable. This forced the surviving men to occupy the few remaining dugouts and this resulted in an uneven occupation of the front with large sections unmanned.' Telephone lines were destroyed, and wire obstacles were swept away. 'The trenches had been levelled completely on wide tracts. No possibility existed for repair work as this would have only resulted in further senseless losses.'

CASUALTIES MOUNT FOR THE BEF

According to the *Statistics of the Military Effort of the British Empire During the Great War*, the total casualties, killed, wounded, prisoners of war and missing, of the BEF between 1 July and 30 November 1916 reached 474,974.

XIII Corps attacked with 18th Division on the left and 30th Division on the right. The latter was on the boundary of 4th Army and when they attacked, Colonel Fairfax from 17th King's went forward arm-in-arm with Commandant Le Petit from the French 153rd Infantry Regiment. The hurricane bombardment of German positions began at 6.25 a.m. here and by 7.30 a.m., with the wire cut and the enemy thoroughly shaken, the troops went forward behind the barrage. On the front of 30th Division, 89th Brigade found little resistance from the enemy and had entered Glatz Redoubt by 8.35 a.m. and taken other strongpoints, having linked up with the French. On the left, 21st Brigade went forward so quickly that the men had to pause to avoid walking into their own barrage. By 8.35 a.m. they had met men from 89th Division and opened the way for the assault on Montauban by 90th Brigade under cover of a smokescreen, and by 11 a.m. the village was in British hands. Pressing on beyond the village, the 16th Manchesters captured the first field guns of the day, which were still in position. By midday, 89th Brigade had seized a flanking position in the brick works and the troops were consolidating the positions, secure in the knowledge that they had taken all of their objectives. The enemy had been pushed back to a depth of over 1,500yd on a broad front and 500 prisoners were taken. The reason for this success is not difficult to establish. Because of command problems and general confusion caused by the effective bombardment, the German troops were not evenly distributed. The small pockets of men were surrounded easily and captured.

On the left of the corps front, 18th Division faced a tougher defensive system, and so entrances to six Russian saps tunnelled under no-man's-land to within 20yd of the German frontline were blown open between 7.15 a.m. and 7.22 a.m. From these entrances

British mortars began a bombardment of the enemy positions to cover the advance. A few minutes later a series of mines, including one of 5,000lb under Casino Point, was blown and in the mining area called 'The Crater Field' a Livens Flame Projector was used to clear the western edge of the defences. On the right 55th Brigade were held up even though, in one of the best-known incidents of the battle, Captain Neville, 8th East Surreys, had kicked off the advance of his company with one of four footballs. An hour later, 30th Division's attack on the right flank allowed the advance to continue. From 10 a.m., the brigade was able to make steady progress until it had reached its ultimate objective, Montauban Alley, in late afternoon. With the full benefit of the mines and flamethrower, 53rd Brigade, in the centre, was able to make rapid progress and had captured the German strongpoint with its three machine guns by 7.50 a.m. With success achieved on both flanks, the brigade pressed forward to meet particularly fierce resistance. It would take until late afternoon to force the Germans back, and it was only following the capture of Montauban village and Pommiers Redoubt that resistance in the centre of the position finally collapsed. By late afternoon all of Montauban Alley, the second objective of 18th Division, was in British hands. By 4 p.m. 18th and 30th Divisions were engaged in consolidating their positions and had established communication with the flanking units, both British and French. Patrols had moved ahead of the captured position and reported that Bernafay and Trône woods were empty. During the course of the evening a German counter-attack from Bernafay Wood was easily repulsed. Despite the success of the corps, casualties were not light; they amounted to over 6,000 men killed, wounded and missing.

MORE POWS 'BEHIND THE WIRE'

During the period from 1 July to 30 December 1916 the BEF captured 832 German officers and 39,375 other ranks, a total of 40,207.

XV Corps – Fricourt and Mametz

This Salient saw the German line turn almost at a right angle to itself, changing from a north–south axis in front of Fricourt to one that was east–west at Mametz. Both villages sat on spurs of land separated by the Willow Stream, which ran behind Fricourt village to the east. The strength of the German position lay in the extensive trench system and the villages, which were exceptionally well fortified. On 1 July there was little artillery opposition as, like elsewhere south of La Boisselle, the Allied artillery had inflicted a good deal of damage on an already weak German artillery force. The principal opposition came from numerous machine gun positions which in many cases where heavily dug-in and mutually supporting.

XV Corps, commanded by Lieutenant General H.S. Horne, consisted of a mix of 'New Army' and regular divisions: in this case 21st (New Army) Division, which was to outflank Fricourt from the north, and 7th (Regular) Division, whose objective was Mametz, which was to link up with 21st Division to the rear of Fricourt, forcing its surrender without a direct assault. The bombardment began, as elsewhere on the British front, at 6.25 a.m., but this was followed by the release of gas at 7.15 a.m. in the German centre, where it was proposed that the British units would wait until a favourable opportunity presented itself before commencing their attack. The gas was followed at 7.26 a.m. by the release of smoke and two minutes later by the firing of three large mines west of Fricourt and other smaller mines elsewhere. The artillery provided a barrage in front of the infantry that provided for a series of 'lifts' ahead of their advance. This variation of the 'creeping barrage' started on the German frontline and did not cover the infantry advance across no-man's-land.

At 7.30 a.m., when the men of 64th Brigade on the left of 21st Division moved into the attack they did so from no-man's-land, having crawled into position during the last few minutes of the bombardment. Despite machine gun fire from La Boisselle, the two leading battalions, their supporting units close behind, got into the enemy frontline and pushed deep into the enemy position. Later waves would not be so fortunate, and heavy casualties were inflicted on the battalions that followed. By 8.45 a.m. the brigade

Men of 7th Division advancing towards Mametz on 1 July. The attackers appear as black specks against the chalk cast up from the trenches. (IWM Q86)

Taken from the same position, this image shows smoke from bursting German shells on the left and a large-calibre shrapnel shell bursting on the right. German artillery caused more casualties than machine guns on 1 July. (IWM Q89)

had reached its objective and awaited support from 63rd Brigade to the south. The latter brigade was not as lucky as its sister unit; it attempted the tactic of sending two companies out to crawl into no-man's-land, but these men were forced back by enemy fire. As a result, the main attack, which began shortly before zero hour, immediately came under increasingly heavy fire. Nevertheless, some elements of the brigade persevered and despite mounting casualties got into the German front and support lines. A second wave at 8.40 a.m. came forward to support this initial success but, under heavy fire from Fricourt Wood, immediately behind the village, the attack on the right faltered. On the left, the brigade was able to link up with 63rd Brigade and 34th Division beyond. By 3.45 p.m., both formations were digging-in, having penetrated the enemy defences to a depth of 1,000yd.

To the south of 63rd Division, facing the three mines in the position called the Tambour in front of Fricourt, was 50th Brigade, which was attached to 21st Division from 17th (Northern) Division. Here two companies of the 7th East Yorkshires attacked with the intention of passing to the north of the mine craters while another battalion of the brigade masked the village. The German defenders both in the area of the Tambour and Fricourt were on the alert and although a few men penetrated the edge of the village, they were driven out by nightfall.

The 7th Division had prepared four Russian saps to close the distance between the British and German frontlines and it was largely down to them that the assault waves managed to break into the German position. The attack was delivered with 22nd Brigade on the left, the 20th in the centre and the 91st on the right. Progress was slow on the left and although the frontline was overwhelmed, only patrols were able to get beyond the German support trenches. On the front of 20th Brigade the contrast was remarkable and although they suffered heavy casualties in no-man's-land, by 7.45 a.m. they had units on the edge of Mametz. Opposition in this area was of variable quality and sporadic. As a result the advance was slow, but steady, and it would not be until around 4 p.m. that Mametz village was cleared and early evening before a firm front had been established facing the Willow Stream.

On the extreme right of the division, 91st Brigade crossed the relatively narrow stretch of no-man's-land under heavy fire. It was able to penetrate rapidly and by 8.15 a.m. was the most advanced of all the troops in the division. After a pause to bring forward reinforcements and reorganise, with the successful men of 18th Division on their right flank, a final push was made just after 2 p.m., which threatened the rear of Mametz and helped lead to the collapse of German resistance in the village. The brigade had covered over 2,500yd in the advance and was now in a position to threaten Fricourt from the rear. Altogether, the corps had captured over 1,600 prisoners, but suffered 8,000 casualties.

III Corps – Ovillers and La Boisselle

The German defences facing III Corps took advantage of the rising ground to the rear of the position and three fingers of high ground that projected towards the British advance. To the north was a spur of land, where the village of Ovillers was located. In the centre of the ridge ran the Roman road from Albert, behind British lines to Bapaume, deep in the German rear; next to the road was the village of La Boisselle. To the south the ground rose up to Fricourt. The topography produced two valleys, one each side of the main road, named on British maps as 'Mash' and 'Sausage'. This area was gently undulating and devoid of natural cover. Standing in the trenches near La Boisselle the German soldier had a view across to the Tara-Usna Hills which hid Albert from view and the maze of British trenches that snaked forward to within only 50yd of the German lines close to the village, but were up to 800yd away elsewhere.

The German defences consisted of a series of deep, well-constructed trenches and dugouts which incorporated the two villages. To the rear, the Thiepval spur rose up towards Pozières to the north. This provided the Germans with ideal observation and firing positions.

The corps commander, Lieutenant General W.P. Pulteney, disposed his two divisions, 8th Division north of the main road and 34th Division south of this boundary. The two divisions were quite different in character, the 8th being regular whilst the 34th was a New Army formation largely recruited from the north-east, especially

This photograph shows members of 34th Division advancing at the double whilst under fire near La Boisselle just after 7.30 a.m. on 1 July. These troops did not get very far before being 'pinned down' by German machine gun fire. (IWM Q52)

Tyneside. Their joint task was to capture the two villages and advance onto the Thiepval spur, threatening the German positions in the north with envelopment. Once established, this dominating position would provide a platform for the next bold thrust by the cavalry for which Haig had optimistically planned.

The preliminary bombardment in this area was hampered by problems with fuses and guns firing short, and well before 1 July it was clear that the destruction of the German defences was far from complete. Two mines had been constructed to deal with specific strongpoints. One, Y Sap, was intended to destroy a position to the north of the main road in La Boisselle, while the second and larger mine, Lochnagar, was situated to the south of the village. Both were fired at 7.28 a.m. and as the dust settled the two divisions left their trenches for the assault. In the north, 8th Division faced a long approach, which the divisional commander had raised as a major problem for his troops. The advance took place with all three brigades in line: 70th Brigade in the north and in contact with 32nd Division, 25th Brigade in the centre with Ovillers as its objective, and 23rd Brigade on the right was to move up Mash Valley to the south of the village. On the left men of the leading waves managed to get into the German positions in the face of heavy fire, but as the volume of machine gun fire increased, especially from the area around Thiepval, later waves were unable to get across no-man's-land. The situation in the centre was similar as the flanking units and men of 25th Brigade had reached the German lines within half an hour, and an hour later attempted to attack the German second-line positions without success. On the right, 23rd Brigade got to within less than 100yd of the trenches in the face of heavy fire from both villages. Despite this sustained machine gun fire, a few men breached the German frontline and hung on for two hours before being driven out in a counter-attack.

This image shows British troops resting and on guard in a captured German trench near La Boisselle. (IWM Q3990)

SHOCK AND AWE

At least one British soldier had his legs broken by the mines detonated on 1 July. He braced himself against both sides of the trench with inevitable consequences.

South of La Boisselle, 34th Division attacked with all three brigades moving off at virtually the same time, 7.35 a.m., but from positions on the frontline for 102nd and 101st Brigades, and the cover of the Tara and Usna hills for 103rd Brigade. Four columns of men moved forward as dots against a green and chalk white background towards the German defences, at the centre of which was the newly created crater of the Lochnagar mine. As the damage caused by the mine explosions was the only element of surprise, the German response was swift. On the left 102nd Brigade, Tyneside Scottish, were given the task of passing to both sides of La Boisselle; 20th and 23rd Battalions of Northumberland Fusiliers managed to reach Y Sap crater, and a few on the far left got to the rear of the village before being driven back. On the right, two further battalions of the same regiment captured Lochnagar Crater and moved well into the German second line before being halted by increasing opposition, including accurate machine gun fire. The 101st Brigade advanced on a narrow front and had a wide section of no-man's-land to cross. Within ten minutes, the leading battalions had suffered 80 per cent casualties. Despite these losses, the units pushed on and the battalions on the right flank, who were in contact with 21st Division, were able to penetrate deep into the German position. The attack was less successful on the left, coming under heavy fire, and when the Royal Scots tried to storm Sausage Redoubt at the head of the valley, they were driven back by a German flamethrower. A few men managed to reach Lochnagar Crater on the left and hung on, and men from three battalions helped to consolidate this position. As the men of 103rd Brigade started their advance down Sausage Valley, leaving their positions on Tara Hill, they immediately came under long-range machine gun fire. Within a few minutes the majority of the brigade were either casualties or pinned down. By 10 a.m.

virtually all movement had stopped and the divisional commander decided that nothing further would be attempted until nightfall, when men from 19th Division would relieve the attacking divisions. Casualties in the corps amounted to over 11,000 and there was little to show for these losses other than the two areas of the German line that remained in British hands.

X Corps – Thiepval

As elsewhere, the German defenders in this area had many advantages over a potential attacker. They had selected the ridge overlooking the valley of the River Ancre and their right flank rested on this obstacle. The village of Thiepval was turned into a fortress and the dominating hill between the village and river became the Schwaben Redoubt. Further south, where the German line turned back to take advantage of the ground, a salient sticking out into no-man's-land had been named after the city of Leipzig. For the British, hemmed in with the river to their backs and little room to deploy in the face of the German trenches, there were few positive features to the position. However, Thiepval Wood, whose trees provided cover from observation, was on a steep slope providing dead ground against which the Germans could not easily bring their artillery to bear. On the extreme right flank of the corps Authuille Wood provided similar natural protection. Elsewhere, the British lines were devoid of cover and under direct enemy observation.

X Corps, under Lieutenant General Sir T.N.L. Morland, consisted of two divisions of quite different character. The one selected to attack north of the village and move towards the Schwaben Redoubt was 36th (Ulster) Division, formed from the Ulster Volunteer Force, an organisation established in 1912 to resist the imposition, as they saw it, of Home Rule in Ireland. Strongly Protestant, the men of the 36th saw themselves as loyal to the Crown, but with a different outlook from the majority of the army. By an ironic twist of fate, 1 July was the anniversary of the Battle of the Boyne in 1690. The second formation in the corps was 32nd Division of Kitchener's New Army. Recruited from the north of England and Glasgow, it combined Kitchener battalions with regulars. This would be both divisions' first battle.

Following an unusually successful preliminary bombardment, the Ulstermen left the edge of Thiepval Wood, where they had been waiting since the previous night. They had formed-up in a maze of specially dug assembly trenches and on a two-brigade front headed for the German defences 300–450yd away uphill. With 109th Brigade on the right and 108th on the left, they found the wire on the forward slope well cut and rapidly broke into the enemy position on the right. The 108th, split either side of the river, were not so successful as they faced heavy flanking fire from the village of St Pierre to the north. By 8.30 a.m. the leading troops of 109th Brigade had advanced over a mile beyond their start line. The 107th Brigade, in reserve, moved forward to exploit the breakthrough achieved by the leading formation just after 9 a.m., but ran into enemy artillery fire and, at one point, due to the speed of their advance, the British barrage. Despite heavy casualties, they pushed on until halted by flanking fire and increasing German opposition. The division found itself isolated as the attack on both flanks had failed, but it held on throughout the day, running increasingly short of ammunition and grenades. By 10.30 that night most of the Ulstermen's gains had been conceded and the Germans re-occupied much of their position.

To the south, the day was not so successful for 32nd Division as for the Ulstermen. On the front of 96th Brigade the contrast could not have been more profound. Here the advance was on the flank of the Ulstermen and the object Thiepval village. As the men of the Northumberland and Lancashire Fusiliers rose from their trenches, they were cut down by fire from the village. A few men angling to the left joined the Ulstermen in the Schwaben Redoubt, but the remainder and their support waves failed to cross no-man's-land in the face of heavy fire. On the division's right flank, the 17th Highland Light Infantry crept to within a few yards of the German frontline at the Leipzig Salient. At zero hour, they rushed the position to find the bulk of the defenders still in their dugouts. More than 300 prisoners were taken. Unable to penetrate beyond the redoubt due to heavy machine gun fire, the men from a variety of units concentrated on consolidation of the position. Elsewhere in this sector the attacks failed due to uncut wire and heavy fire. All attempts to reinforce the men in the German positions led to heavy casualties. Some men did get through and by mid-afternoon attempts were made to push on into the German position, but opposition was too strong and the attacks failed with further losses. By the end of the day, the division had a toehold in the redoubt, their only reward for a bloody day. Total casualties amounted to over 9,000 men.

VIII Corps – Beaumont-Hamel and Serre

The topography of this area clearly favoured the defenders. The German trench line ran along the spurs of high ground on which sat the village of Serre, across Redan Ridge, and then in front of the village of Beaumont-Hamel, ending on the banks of the River Ancre at Beaucourt in the south. This position offered poor observation for the British and had the advantage of areas of 'dead ground' for the Germans against which it was difficult to direct artillery fire. With high ground to the rear of their position, German troops had direct observation well into the British lines. Months of back-breaking toil by the German troops had done much to improve the already favourable position and the villages of Serre and Beaumont-Hamel, Y Ravine and the dominant Hawthorn Ridge had been turned into miniature fortresses, each of which would need to be dealt with by the attackers. At the Heidenkopf, south of Serre, called the Quadrilateral by the British, the defenders of 121st Reserve Regiment had realised that the position, which jutted forward into no-man's-land, was vulnerable to attack and four defensive mines were laid in front of the parapet. The intention was to blow the 'mine field' as the British closed on the position. In the north no-man's-land was up to 500yd wide, but around Beaumont-Hamel the distance was shorter, in some cases no more than 150yd.

With these defences to overcome, Lieutenant General Sir Aylmer Hunter-Weston, commanding VIII Corps, decided to use all but a small part of the four divisions available to him and assault Serre, Redan Ridge and Beaumont-Hamel simultaneously. Facing the well-organised defences around Beaumont-Hamel was 29th Division. This was the last of the regular divisions raised and had earned the name 'The Incomparable 29th' for their performance at Gallipoli. The plan of attack developed for the 29th employed great military ingenuity and took advantage of the few weaknesses in the German defensive plan. It was recognised that two features of the defences would threaten any assault on Beaumont-Hamel. On the right was the redoubt on Hawthorn Ridge whence the defenders could fire into the flanks of any attacking troops. It was therefore decided to tunnel from the British lines and lay a mine under this strongpoint. This mine, built by 252 Tunnelling Company Royal Engineers and charged with 40,000lb of explosives, would destroy the German defences and produce a crater. The redoubt could then be captured by an assault party to provide an excellent vantage point for British troops. From here, they would be able to dominate both the approaches to the village and the flanking German defences. As an additional measure, it was agreed that the troops who would attack the village would do so not from the British trenches, but from a sunken lane, a feature that lay in no-man's-land. This would reduce the distance to be covered and had the benefit of surprise. To get these troops into the sunken lane a Russian sap was constructed and B and D Companies of 1st Lancashire Fusiliers plus four Stokes mortars moved into the sunken lane before dawn via the tunnel from the frontline. The firing of the mine is the most controversial aspect of the operation on the front of 29th Division that day. In other areas, the mines were fired at 7.28 a.m., but at Hawthorn Ridge, due to a fear of casualties amongst the attackers, the mine was fired at 7.20 a.m. In addition, the main British barrage then lifted away from the German frontline, not only near the mine, but also along the entire divisional frontage.

The British bombardment had caused a great deal of damage to the defences in this area. A German observer reported that the preliminary bombardment was quite destructive:

> On the right wing of the regiment where the hillside descended toward Auchonvillers the dugouts were crushed, craters appeared 3 meters deep and 4-5 meters across. The wire was badly damaged and the trenches were levelled in many places. Many dugout entrances across the line were damaged and blocked requiring work to keep them open.

However, as the moment for the attack drew closer,

Everything was made battle ready, everything was strapped on, the rifle was grasped and hand grenades were in the right place. The Officers and Other Ranks waited on the stairways and in the dugouts ready for the defence for the moment when the enemy fire was transferred to the rear.

When the attack came, 'Telephone and red light balls called for help from the artillery. The infantry and machine gun fire mowed down the attackers so that they soon hesitated and threw themselves down.'

Initially the operation, by 86th Brigade, went reasonably well and although some German shells fell around the sunken lane there was little evidence that the defences were on a high state of alert. Promptly at 7.20 a.m., the mine was fired and Geoffrey Malins, the official cinematographer in this area, captured the moment on film. As the debris settled two platoons of 2nd Royal Fusiliers rushed the crater with four machine guns and four Stokes mortars. At the same time the mortars in the sunken lane began a hurricane bombardment of the German wire and trenches. At 7.30 a.m., with British heavy bombardment moving to targets deeper in German lines, the main attack began. Once again, despite all the careful preparation and rehearsal, the plans began to fail almost at once. Within a few moments of the mine's detonation, members of the German garrison, recognising the significance of the feature, rushed to capture the crater. Heavy fire from the flanks meant that although the mortars and machine guns with the party from the Royal Fusiliers reached the near side of the crater, most of the men carrying ammunition were hit. Meanwhile, attacking from the sunken lane, B and D companies of the Lancashire Fusiliers were cut down by fire from ahead and also from the area of the crater. Only about fifty reached the dip in no-man's-land and were then unable to advance. At the same time, a platoon of B Company attacked south of Beaumont Road and more men from 2nd Royal Fusiliers reached the crater. Subsequently 16th Middlesex attacked, but fewer than 120 men reached the crater. Around 10.30 a.m., under fierce counter-attack and short of ammunition, resistance in Hawthorn Crater collapsed and the survivors returned to British lines.

'SEE YOU ON THE OTHER SIDE?'

The Battle of the Somme began with an attack on a
17-mile front in which 110,000 British infantrymen went
'over the top'.

On the right flank, at 7.30 a.m., men from 87th Brigade, including 2nd South Wales Borderers, headed for Y Ravine. Only a few got within 100yd of the German frontline because of heavy fire. On the far right, the 1st Inniskilling Fusiliers were more successful and broke into the enemy position, but were driven out by a fierce counter-attack. White flares fired from the German lines suggested that the attack on this front had been completed and in the next hour and a half two waves of men from the supporting brigades went forward to be met by machine gun and artillery fire. Those who survived hid in the numerous shell holes and awaited darkness to return to their own lines. The most tragic action on this front occurred just after 9 a.m. Despite desperate attempts to stop the movement, 1st Newfoundland Regiment, who were unable to move through the trenches because they were so clogged with wounded men, advanced from third-line trenches and lost 710 men in a matter of minutes. Few reached no-man's-land and most fell within British lines.

To the north of 29th Division was 4th Division, another regular formation, which went into action on a narrow, single-brigade, front with the objectives of the Heidenkopf on the left and the forward slope of Redan Ridge on the right. As elsewhere that morning, the troops' movement into no-man's-land provoked an immediate response from the defenders. The German positions had been heavily damaged by the preliminary bombardment, which mainly consisted of 18lb shrapnel shells, but the garrison from 121st Reserve Regiment were able to man their trenches. They commenced firing into the British advance. The fighting that followed was bitter, but in some areas the British troops were successful. The decision had been made to avoid a direct assault on the Heidenkopf and the attacking units outflanked its defences, rapidly breaking into the main German trench line. Though the mines had killed some British troops, men from the leading battalions established themselves in a position over about 600yd. However, on the right flank the 1st East Lancashires and second wave 1st Hampshires found the wire largely uncut and were halted in no-man's-land.

In response to the assault, German artillery fire had begun to fall in no-man's-land and the British troops took heavy casualties from the combined fire of the machine guns on Redan Ridge and increasingly from Serre. Under fire from three sides and with the British bombardment now falling ineffectually far ahead of the troops it was meant to support, the men in and around the Heidenkopf were in an unenviable position. Reinforced by the second wave, who had taken heavy casualties crossing no-man's-land, there was little room for manoeuvre, the majority of the senior officers were dead or wounded and there was no way to communicate with the rear. Information from contact patrols of the RFC about the situation was ambiguous and the decision was taken at about 8.35 a.m. to halt the support battalions from 10th and 12th Brigades. This message reached some units but not others. Following their timetable, at 9.30 a.m. battalions moved off towards the Heidenkopf to be met by a hurricane of enemy fire. Few reached their objective.

Aware that his most northerly division would form 4th Army's flank, Haig planned for it to wheel at right angles to the axis of advance once it had broken into the enemy position to provide the protection needed for the other two and a half divisions of the corps. The division he chose for this task was 31st, recruited from the industrial northern towns and including a number of Pals battalions. This was to be their first battle and the men were optimistic of success. Attempts to tunnel into no-man's-land were largely unsuccessful so it was decided that the two brigades should move into no-man's-land and be in position by 7.20 a.m. in order to close the distance to be covered in the attack. At the appointed time, 94th Brigade, on the left, moved off uphill from the line of copses named after the Gospels which marked the British frontline.

It was clear almost at once that the operation was not going to plan. The smoke intended to screen the flank failed to develop, and the attackers found themselves under machine gun fire within a few minutes of moving off. What followed was confused and bloody.

In some places small groups of the attackers reached the German trenches and engaged in bitter hand-to-hand fighting as they tried to advance into the position. One small party of 11th East Lancashire Regiment reached Serre, but, without reinforcements, it was wiped out. On the front of 93rd Brigade the men advanced into heavy fire and after about fifteen minutes forward movement became impossible. Despite the odds, one group from 18th Durham Light Infantry reached Pendant Copse, nearly 2,000yd from their starting point. It was all in vain though; casualties were so heavy that some battalions were virtually wiped out. The division had lost over 3,600 men and totally failed to achieve its objectives. Critically, as the fighting around Serre ground to a standstill, the German defenders there were able to divert their attention to the attack developing to the south.

Despite optimistic reports of British troops being observed in Serre, Pendant Copse and Y Ravine, the attack of XIII Corps had been a disaster. Hasty plans to reinforce these apparent successes were called off by mid-afternoon and the area around the Heidenkopf was largely abandoned as the survivors gradually filtered back across no-man's-land. By the end of the day the scale of the disaster was becoming clear: 14,000 men had been lost with nothing to show for it.

3rd Army

Gommecourt

VII Corps

There was a 2-mile gap between the units of 3rd Army (General Sir Edmund Allenby) that attacked at Gommecourt and those of 4th Army (Rawlinson) north of Serre. The intention of the operation at Gommecourt, the northernmost of those planned for Z Day, was to provide a diversion, drawing artillery fire and reinforcements away from the attacks in the south. At the same time, it was hoped that, as an additional bonus, the operation would remove the bulge in the German line that projected into British lines. Two territorial divisions from VII Corps, commanded by Lieutenant General Snow, were selected for this task. The left-hand, and hence most northerly, of

A German cross erected over the body of Captain Lewes from the Notts and Derby Regiment (Sherwood Foresters). His divisional attack at Gommecourt was one of the disasters of 1 July. (IWM Q7797)

the divisions was 46th (North Midland) whilst the other was 56th (London). The plan called for their attacks to be delivered into the flanks of the Salient and then to converge at the rear of Gommecourt village. The artillery programme called for this position to be reached at 8 a.m. This was seen as a means of 'pinching out' the formidable German defences, which enjoyed the benefit of favourable ground with good observation and concealment in woodland. The 2,000yd gap between the two divisions was to be screened by units that were not attacking, but the wire would be cut and smoke used as elsewhere on this front. The defences in the Salient, which were already formidable, had been strengthened as the preparations for the assault had not gone unnoticed by the Germans. In addition to the fixed defences, the garrison of the Salient was reinforced by three regiments, nine battalions of infantry. This was part of the British plan to draw German resources away from the more important action further south both before the battle and on Z Day. In late June General Snow, commander of VII Corps, told Haig with no little pride that 'They know we are coming all right.'

To the south of Gommecourt, 56th Division made their attack. On this frontage, the battalions of 168th and 169th Brigades were more successful, starting their attack from closer to the German frontline and having the benefit of surprise. They also made use of the smoke and found to their relief that the barbed wire was well cut. This was partly due to the Bangalore Torpedoes – tubes stuffed with explosives – that had been used the previous night. In some areas, the German defenders emerged from their dugouts too slowly and were captured. Over 300 unwounded prisoners were sent to the rear, but when a number were killed by their own shelling, the remainder were kept in numerous dugouts. Other German soldiers still in uncaptured dugouts were by-passed by the Londoners and emerged to fire on the British from the rear and obstruct reinforcements. Despite the confusion in their wake, the men of 56th Division pushed on through the first two lines of trenches, penetrating well into the enemy position. By now, the division had reached many of its objectives but found increased resistance to further advances. This resistance was centred on Kern Redoubt, which the Germans had built for this very eventuality. Though a courageous group fought through the German lines to effect the anticipated junction with men of the 46th, they were disappointed. No members of that division were to reach Gommecourt except as prisoners.

Here, as on the frontage of 46th Division, their gains were threatened. German artillery fire, which was heavy and more effective in this sector than any other part of the front, barred British troops from crossing no-man's-land. Reinforcements and much-needed ammunition, specifically grenades, could not be brought forward. The men of the two brigades were looking over their shoulders for assistance that would never arrive. Worse still, the failure of 46th Division's attack to the north meant that the Germans could turn their full attention and effective counter-attacks on the men of the 56th who had a 'toehold' in the Salient. With no target on their flanks, the German artillery could concentrate on the men holding out in the positions they had captured in the German trench lines.

Under the protection of a heavy smokescreen 46th Division made their assault on a frontage of two brigades, 137th and 139th. The smokescreen began to develop around 7.15; by 7.30 it was so thick in front of 46th Division's assembly trenches that when they attacked they had great difficultly maintaining direction. Worse still, despite the careful preparation, the wire was found to be largely uncut and even those lanes that had been made were difficult to spot. German troops manned their parapets even before zero hour as their observers had seen groups of British troops moving to their assault positions. Supporting British troops where unable to fire for fear of hitting their own men and, as the bombardment moved forward, the men of both brigades were left isolated. The British artillery fire, which amounted to a virtual creeping barrage, moved forward strictly following the timetable of lifts as the infantry fell behind. The German defenders had no inhibitions about firing into no-man's-land even if no targets were visible. Artillery, machine guns and rifles poured heavy fire into the British and only a few members of 137th Brigade on the right of 46th Division made it to the German frontline. The 139th did a little better and got men into the German trenches, but they were too few to go further, trying instead to consolidate their positions. However, they discovered that the German bombardment falling in no-man's-land left them cut off from their reinforcements and increasingly vulnerable to counter-attacks, which developed rapidly. Throughout the day these men held onto the lodgement they had captured, anxiously awaiting relief.

Secondary attacks were proposed on the front of 46th Division in support of the men in the Salient, but shortages of ammunition, general confusion and the collapse of communications meant they did not happen. The British troops were gradually driven out of the German position. By dusk the last of them had been driven back to the British lines. Casualties ran to 4,300 in 56th Division and 2,455 for 46th Division. This latter is the lowest of any of the divisions that attacked on 1 July; the figures in part reflect the impossibility of their task. The divisional commander, Major General the Hon. E.J. Montague-Stuart-Wortley, decided to call off the attacks planned for later in the day when it became all too apparent that they would be futile.

Opposite: With the battle having moved on, these British soldiers can rest in the remains of a German trench system near Ovilliers. Note, however, that the dugout entrance has survived the bombardment. (IWM Q4123)

The German Experience

For many German soldiers the initial response to the events of 1 July was relief. The long wait enduring continual shelling was over and the end of the bombardment allowed them to prepare for the long-awaited attack. In some areas, the German troops were rapidly overwhelmed, but in many others, they marvelled at the spectacle that unfolded before them that bright summer's morning. Despite local surprise at the bombardment and the mines detonated under their positions, German troops proved adept at launching immediate counter-attacks to seize key features. They appeared behind the attackers as they emerged from dugouts and used their local knowledge to exploit the topography to maximum effect. Notable that day was the leadership demonstrated by relatively junior German soldiers. Although the German army operated with a smaller number of officers than the British, their highly trained NCOs showed great initiative and tactical ability. Their losses during the protracted battle would have a profound effect on future operations.

This German artillery unit has been hit by the British bombardment near Mountauban. The artillery preparations were most successful in the southern sector. (IWM Q674)

Whereas the units facing the French and XIII Corps found their defences crumbled under the weight of enemy artillery and their own supporting weapons were largely silenced, the defenders in the northern sector had time to pick targets carefully, demonstrating superb fire discipline and causing horrific casualties. However, the German army did not have an easy day; their casualties mounted rapidly, adding to the hundreds lost during the preliminary bombardment. German casualties were not compiled on a daily basis and the confusion of the day means that accurate figures are elusive. Nonetheless, estimates for German casualties, including prisoners, range from 10,000 to 12,000 – considerably less than the British, but the situation for German High Command was not entirely favourable by the end of 1 July.

As we have seen, some reserves had already been called forward the previous month and in many areas new batteries were in place. The German forces on the Somme were not well provisioned with additional reserves and some piecemeal reorganisation was taking place when the attack was launched. Even before Z Day some areas of the German defensive line were very weak and vulnerable. At 6th Army headquarters news from the front was initially received in a calm, calculated manner, and General von Below's only real concern was the fall of the Schwaben Redoubt. Later in the day von Below heard that General von Stein, commanding XIV Reserve Corps, had been forced by shelling to leave his headquarters in Bapaume. Communications were broken, and when re-established appeared to indicate that a collapse in the southern sectors was imminent. Any loss of ground was met by channelling all available reserves and attempting to restrict the loss to a minimum. Sometimes even grooms, cooks and servants were sent into action.

The lack of any real British success in the north allowed the Germans to concentrate on the southern portion of the battle and to rearrange the reinforcements as needed. The German fixed positions in some areas were badly damaged; further south towards the Somme much of the first line had been taken and numerous guns were out of action or captured. This was the area of greatest concern. At the end of the day the situation was reviewed, the placement of troops was established and reserves were called forward to fill gaps and reinforce the lines where the need was greatest. The true picture would not be known until 2 July at least, but in the first few days after Z Day the German position from Montauban south to the Somme was virtually broken and they had lost over 100 guns. The line held though, and the professional German soldier stood his ground as best he could. There was elation in some sectors when the fighting was over and the Germans realised how well most of the line had held and how many men the British had lost.

The Situation at the End of the Day

The Gommecourt diversionary action was a failure and the heavy casualties around Serre and Beaumont-Hamel testified to the German army's success in the face of the British plan of attack. Critically, however, the latter had had some success in the northern sector. The 4th Division had broken through the German frontline and had got well into their second line. Although 29th Division had ended the day on its start line, the Ulstermen of 36th Division to their south had done a superb job, capturing the Schwaben Redoubt and penetrating

As the advance continues, the field guns are brought forward and this 18-pounder has been in action for some time judging by the number of empty cases on the right and the 'stripped down' gunners. (IWM Q4066)

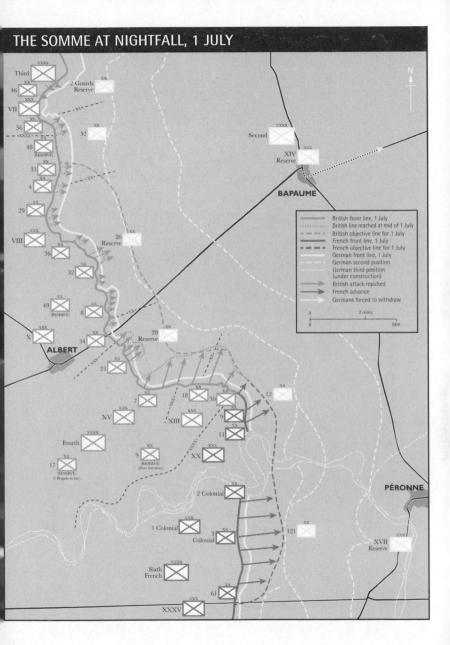

THE SOMME AT NIGHTFALL, 1 JULY

Third
46
VII
56
48 RESERVE
31
4
29
VIII
36
32
49 RESERVE
8
X
34
ALBERT
21
7
XV
Fourth
17 RESERVE (1 Brigade in line)
9 RESERVE (Does not move)
XX
2 Colonial
1 Colonial
3 Colonial
Sixth French
61
XXXV

2 Guards Reserve
52
26 Reserve
28 Reserve
18
XIII
30
9
11
12
121
Second
XIV Reserve
BAPAUME
PÉRONNE
XVII Reserve

British front line, 1 July
British line reached at end of 1 July
British objective line for 1 July
French front line, 1 July
French objective line for 1 July
German front line, 1 July
German second position
German third position (under construction)
British attack repulsed
French advance
Germans forced to withdraw

0   2 miles
0   5km

almost as far as Grandcourt. To the south elements of 32nd Division got into the Leipzig Salient but no further. Like the successful units further north, they were unsupported on either flank. Having crossed no-man's-land, British units found that the German defensive bombardment, which fell behind them, between the British and German trenches, cut them off from supplies and reinforcements. North of the Bapaume–Albert road, 32nd and 36th Divisions had established toeholds in the German defences. Over the course of the day and into the evening the narrow gains in the German frontline were eaten into by German counter-attacks and eventually the positions were abandoned.

The situation to the south of the Bapaume–Albert road was far more favourable. The Allies had been able to exploit weakness in the German defences, and combined greater weight of artillery and better planning to produce a military triumph. III Corps had suffered heavy casualties, but was now established in the German first-line positions at Ovillers. XV Corps had achieved partial success, moving to outflank Fricourt having captured Mametz. It was a day of triumph for XIII Corps. Despite heavy casualties, the corps had taken most of its initial objectives, including Montauban. On the right flank, the French were even more successful, moving onto the German second-line positions. The attack in the north shattered and, as news of the achievements in the south reached headquarters, Rawlinson failed to order the available reserves into action. Haig believed there was an opportunity to exploit what he took to be a potential breach in the enemy defences, but Rawlinson was still working on his programme of 'bite and hold'. Although total collapse of the German army between Mametz and the Somme was unlikely, Rawlinson did try to exploit his forces' success. Objectives that were undefended during the first few days of July would be fought for in bloody battles in the weeks ahead. The scene was set for the bloody struggle that would follow over the next 148 days on the Somme.

The Somme 2 July to 13 November

1–13 July	Battle of Albert
2 July	Capture of Fricourt
2–6 July	Capture of La Boiselle
9–13 July	Capture of Mametz Wood and Contalmaison
11–12 July	Germans suspend operations at Verdun
14–17 July	Battle of Bazentin Ridge
14 July	Dawn attack on Trône Wood, Longueval and High Wood; cavalry in action
15–17 July	Capture of Ovillers and battle for Delville Wood begins – ends on 3 September
19 July	Diversionary attack at Fromelles north of the Somme
18–22 July	Attacks at Longueval, Delville and High Woods
23 July	Battle for Poziers begins – ends on 3 September
3–6 September	Battle of Guillemont
9 September	Battle of Ginchy
15–23 September	Battle of Flers-Courcelette – begins with first ever tank attack
25–28 September	Battle of Morval on boundary between British and French forces
26–28 September	Battle of Thiepval – concludes with the capture of the Thiepval position which had resisted all attacks since 1 July
1–18 October	Battle of Le Transloy Ridge
1 October–11 November	Battle of the Ancre Heights
13–18 November	Battle of the Ancre and capture of Beaumont-Hamel

1916

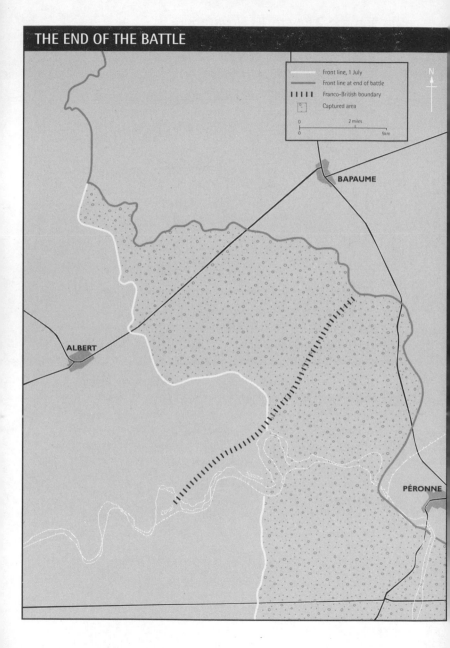

THE END OF THE BATTLE

Front line, 1 July
Front line at end of battle
Franco-British boundary
Captured area

0   2 miles
0   5km

N

BAPAUME

ALBERT

PÉRONNE

A Monument in Private Hands

The Butte de Warlencourt is owned by the Western Front Association and can be visited by the public.

The British casualties for the first day of the battle numbered 57,470, of whom 19,240 were killed and 2,152 missing. This was the bloodiest day in the entire history of the British army. British pre-battle estimates indicated that the BEF could expect approximately 40,000 causalities – clearly an underestimate. German casualties on the front are estimated to have been around 6,000; a further 2,000 were lost as prisoners. There is a clear mathematical imbalance and although the full compilation of British casualties would take weeks there was no suggestion from General Haig, or later the politicians, that the battle would be called off. Although the figures are collectively shocking and devastated the families who were to receive news of their losses over forthcoming weeks, the international political imperative and military situation that had led to the battle meant that the British army would have to continue the task it had been given. If little had been achieved on the first day, it was vital to maintain pressure on the Germans in order to achieve a more decisive result. Critical to this opinion was the attitude of the French, the senior military partner in the coalition. Many French civilians and members of the armed forces saw British casualties, which were still minor compared to their own, as evidence that the United Kingdom was beginning to play a part in the struggle that was more reflective of her manpower and industrial and naval might.

It is clear from the first day of the Somme that British troops had much to learn about the reality of trench warfare, one example being the failure of advancing troops to effectively 'clear' German positions they overran. They either simply passed them or threw a few grenades into the dugout entrances. This would have worked in shallow British positions, but German dugouts were 3ft deep and had multiple entrances, enabling the garrison to appear behind the attackers and engage them from the rear. Another aspect of the first day was the effect of German defensive artillery fire. Despite the belief that most casualties were caused by machine guns that day, artillery was the big killer. As the British attacked, German defenders sent up flares that indicated the need for the guns to open fire. This fire was directed at no-man's-land between the German and British trenches for it was across this open space littered with obstacles that the attackers would have to cross to reach the German frontline. Thus, although the leading waves of troops may have got into the German position, the defensive fire effectively cut them off from support. The advancing British were forced to push into the German trenches engaging in bitter grenade battles as the defenders counter-attacked. The first wave of British had equipment, food, water, weapons and ammunition for a limited period. Although there was sufficient food on the day, hot water became scarce, as did grenades. Carrying parties had been detailed to follow the first waves into the enemy positions, but all along the front these troops suffered heavy casualties as they moved off even though they were now behind friendly troops. One brigade bombing officer of 56th Division spent the day organising parties to take bombs forward only to see these men killed or wounded before they were able to deliver their much-needed bags and boxes of grenades. Elsewhere, this battle to reinforce the frontline went on into the night and 36th (Ulster) Division attempted to dig communication trenches to bridge no-man's-land. Under indirect artillery fire and direct machine gun fire, these attempts, as elsewhere, failed. In many areas the successful advance was ultimately hampered by lack of ammunition rather than the allegedly crippling weight of their packs.

The days following 1 July were not repeats of the first if for no other reason than it had taken months to plan this assault and the logistical effort to build up ammunition and stores had been a monumental task. Time would be required to achieve anything like the same effort again. It can be argued that, logistically, had the German army collapsed on the first day, it would have been almost impossible for the existing railway system and road network to support a triumphant Allied pursuit. The campaign that followed comprised periods of localised fighting involving one or two divisions. This was followed by subsequent set-piece efforts when the men, ammunition and stores were ready for another push. This drawn out campaign presented evidence of improved tactics and training, the use of new methods of war demonstrated by the first employment of tanks in mid-September. Professor Gary Sheffield described this process as 'the learning curve', which he revised to 'the learning Loch Ness Monster'. This is because as the British improved their tactics and methods of waging war so the German army made similar changes reflecting their improved understanding of the fighting and of British tactics. It cannot be said that the British high command demonstrated an outstanding grasp of this new warfare and it is true that many casualties were caused by poor planning and staff work, inconsistent development of new tactics and, at times, a lack of imagination. However, the German generals managed to achieve significant 'own goals'. Perhaps the most obvious example is the standing order that all ground lost to the enemy should be retaken by counter-attack 'even to the use of the last man'. This policy was only changed to a more flexible form of defensive tactics when the loss of life had become critical. The new doctrines imposed by the arrival of Generals Hindenburg and Ludendorff in late August reflected a realisation that German casualties could not be supported at previous levels. Within a month, the status of the Somme led Hindenburg to classify that front as all-important and to order the construction of the *Siegfried Stellung*, the 'Hindenburg Line' to the Allies.

The campaign on the Somme was fought through the summer and autumn and only ended when wet winter weather put a stop to all efforts in mid-November. According to one account of the campaign, Captain E.A. James' *Record of the Battles and Engagements*, the campaign can be divided into the Battle of Albert (the nearest large town to the action) between 1 and 13 July, and the diversionary attack on Gommecourt on the 1st. Most of this action has been dealt with previously, as has the reason why the campaign was not called off despite the losses of the first day. After 1 July, Haig reorganised the command structure on the Somme. General Gough was appointed commander of X and VIII Corps, on the northern front, previously under Rawlinson. Gough's Reserve Army thus took control of the northern sector, the least successful area on the first day. Gough felt unable to conduct offensive operations until 3 July, but the situation further south was far more positive. On 4th Army's front German counter-attacks near Montauban were beaten off with artillery fire. Fricourt fell on 2 July and La Boisselle the next day. An attack on the position at Thiepval by 32nd Division on the 3rd failed. Although patrols further south found that positions in the woods at Mametz were unoccupied, when an attempt was made to take them the following day, the Germans had reoccupied them. Elsewhere, Bernafay Wood and Caterpillar Wood were taken. By this stage it had been agreed by Haig and Joffre that future operations would concentrate on the area of success in the south while Gough's Reserve Army in the north occupied German forces on its front to prevent them deploying as reinforcements elsewhere. The value of the old military maxim of not reinforcing failure was clear to all involved. For this reason it was decided that the objective would be the German second-line positions running along the higher ground from Longueval and Bazentin-le-Petit. The first few days of July demonstrate a lack of unified policy or 'thrust' between the British and the French to the south. Positions that would take months to capture later in the campaign lay under- or undefended and the brief respite of these crucial days allowed the Germans to reorganise and dig-in on ground of their choosing. German soldiers were always willing to get to work with pickaxe and shovel and they used the opportunity to turn the areas of woodland into defended works for which the then still existing tree canopy provided natural camouflage. In the period up to 14 July the 17th (Northern) and 38th (Welsh) Divisions attempted to attack the area of Contalmaison and Mametz Wood and gains were made near the ruins of the village of Ovillers. By 10 July Contalmaison was in the hands of 23rd and 38th Divisions and they had finally secured Mametz Wood, although with heavy losses. The scene was set for the next set-piece action: the Battle of Bazentin.

MISSING IN ACTION

The monument to the missing at Thiepval lists the names of 72,000 men whose remains were not found or identified after the Battle of the Somme.

This battle based on XV and XIII Corps was very different from 1 July. There was no prolonged preliminary bombardment heralding the offensive; instead it was possible to achieve complete surprise. Five minutes was considered sufficient, although efforts were made to locate enemy gun positions so that counter battery fire could reduce German defensive fire when the attack was launched. As the artillery plan began at 3.20 a.m. and the infantry attack only five minutes later, the whole first phase of the operation commenced in the dark, the infantry attack occurring at dawn. As on 1 July, in some areas troops crawled out into no-man's-land to narrow the distance to the enemy positions pre-attack, and 7th, 21st and 3rd Divisions carried all their objectives. On the right flank, 9th (Scottish) Division were able to establish themselves on the edge of Delville Wood and 18th Division demonstrated their usual flair in capturing Trône Wood.

Indian cavalry wait to advance. The number of horses in use for both cavalry and transport hints at the logistics required to support the BEF.

A captured German trench in Delville Wood. Note that despite the shattered trees the trench has partly survived. Together with the dugouts it can still shelter men from fire.

By mid-morning over 6,000yd of the German second line was in British hands. The contrast with the operation conducted only two weeks earlier was startling. Critical to the success was the weight of fire used by British artillery. General Rawlinson had two-thirds of the number of guns available on 1 July, but they were used to fire shells at a frontage of 6,000yd rather than the 2,000yd previously. The German positions took at least five times as many hits as on 1 July. However, again the initial triumph was not fully exploited. Rawlinson's plan called for 2nd Indian Cavalry Division, which included both British and Indian units, to exploit the infantry's success. It must be remembered that British cavalry of this period were armed with the same rifle as the infantry and had a high proportion of machine guns and the necessary ammunition, which a mounted crew with packhorses could move forward far more quickly than infantry. Communication difficulties combined with problems of finding suitable routes meant that the cavalry were not in action until late in the day. Although there was some mounted action close to High Wood in which cavalry with lances routed German infantry, the end of the battle came with a machine gun duel between cavalry guns and Germans on the fringe of Delville Wood. Cavalry casualties were remarkably light as they were able to use speed and surprise to advance before sending the bulk of the vulnerable horses to the rear. By the end of the day High Wood and Delville Wood were still in enemy hands although 7th Division was established on the fringe of the former.

In the days that followed, fighting continued in the area of Delville Wood and Longueval, with South African Brigade and 9th Division involved in bitter conflict. The subsequent battle inspired the men to rename the area 'Devil's Wood'. The trees shattered by artillery, rotting corpses and a maze of trenches were disputed for two months by different units, between 15 July and 3 September. Further north a similar battle occurred for High Wood and fighting swayed back and forth among the ruins of the Great Wood on the ridge between 20 and 25 July. This phase of the campaign was characterised by the small size of operations, often no more than a few companies

The battlefield near Thiepval in September. By this time the village and château were shattered ruins and the chalky ground was cut up by trenches.

at a time. The exception was an ambitious night attack planned for 22–23 July. Six British divisions mounted an assault in concert with the French on the eastern flank at Guillemont, on a line that ended at Pozières in the north, but the French failed to attack and artillery support was inadequate. Worse still, the time of attack was not co-ordinated and the divisions found that the enemy had largely abandoned fixed trench positions for improvised shelter in shell holes, which were difficult to identify and for the artillery to destroy. Each side was learning, but success in one action did not guarantee future success and divisions already held in high regard, such as the 19th, 30th and 51st, failed in the attack. Inevitably, casualties mounted and by mid-September 4th Army had suffered 82,000 men killed, wounded or missing, with little to show for it in terms of ground captured.

Some modern historians have suggested that this is the point at which General Haig should have called off the 'Big Push', which had clearly failed to either achieve a breakthrough or crush the Germans' will to fight. However, reverses in one sector were matched by success elsewhere. On the same day as the unsuccessful operation by 4th Army, two divisions of Gough's Reserve Army were able to capture the village of Pozières, which sat astride the Roman road between Albert and Bapaume. A well-planned dawn attack, supported by good artillery by 48th (South Midland) Division on the left of the road and 1st Australian Division on the right, captured the village and ridge on which it sat. The advance created a salient into the German position and British/Australian troops were now behind the Germans who still held the position at Thiepval and threatened other positions to the south. The success of the 23rd led to the piecemeal commitment of other Australian units in the fighting around the village, The Battle of Pozières ended on 8 August, by which time the Australians had suffered heavy casualties. But this did not conclude operations in this area; three Australian divisions, 1st, 2nd and 4th, suffered 23,000 casualties in six weeks attempting to advance towards Mouquet Farm between Pozières and Thiepval. Despite this action the Thiepval defences shrugged off attacks by 25th and 48th Divisions in late August and subsequent operations by British divisions, and 4th Australian Division failed to achieve any major success.

A Vickers machine gun team in action (clearly a posed photograph). The men are wearing the P.H. gas helmet and the machine gun is fitted with a Sangster auxiliary tripod. This miniature tripod was intended to allow the gun to come into action even when the heavy tripod was not available.

The small-scale actions which followed were largely 'line straightening' operations intended to prepare positions for the set-piece Battle of Flers-Courcelette planned for mid-September. Operations around Guillemont, intended to demonstrate Anglo-French co-operation, were frustrated by the weather (it rained heavily in mid-August) and by differences in outlook between Haig and Foch. There were some successes in these operations and reliance was increasingly placed on artillery barrages and the use of machine guns in support of infantry action. During 33rd Division's attack in the area of Delville and High Wood on 24 August, 100th Company of the Machine Gun Corps fired one box (250 rounds) less than 1 million rounds to isolate the German position from support or retreat. Nevertheless, fighting continued in this heavily disputed and strategic area. Guillemont was finally captured in early September and Ginchy was capture by 16th (Irish) Division on 9 September. The official historian of the British army called the advance 'slow and costly'; both terms which can be applied to the entire Somme battle to that point. To the south the French advance continued at a slightly better rate, but with heavy casualties. The British forces were not yet ready for an operation which saw the advent of a new weapon in the history of warfare.

Dust, not mud. Field cookers in Sausage Valley near La Boisselle in September. As there was one cooker per company, this must be the cooking area for part of a brigade. Note the number of transport horses needed to supply men at the front.

The Battle of Flers-Courcelette was a set-piece operation which began on 15 September and ended on the 22nd. This battle saw both New Zealand and Canadian divisions committed and the successful first employment of the tank. Developed in secret by the 'Land Ship Committee', the tank, as it was codenamed, was intended to overcome the problems faced by infantry in crossing trenches and barbed wire whilst under fire from machine guns. The vehicle had a crew of six, was armed with either two 6-pounder guns and machine guns (the male), or just machine guns (the female). The vehicle was armoured against rifle and machine gun fire and operated on tracks that could cope with uneven ground, crush barbed wire and cross trenches. Conditions for the crew inside the vehicle, with an exposed engine and uncertain ventilation, were difficult and the Mark I tanks were slow and mechanically unreliable. However, they offered the infantry support with firepower, destroyed strongpoints and could advance protected from virtually all enemy small arms. On 15 September only forty-eight tanks were available and of these just over a dozen were able to join the attack that morning as others had simply broken down. They were brought forward to their 'battle positions' in the dark to maintain the element of surprise. However,

Rawlinson chose to spread the 'runners' along the front of the attack, but also to include in his artillery plan 'lanes' for the tanks which were not to be shelled for fear of obstructing them. These decisions, and that to commit the tank to battle 'early', before it had been improved or was available in larger numbers, remain controversial.

The battle was, like 1 July, an ambitious operation fought on a front from the Reserve Army, across all of 4th Army and down to the French area, where the 6th Army also attacked. Haig's preference was to use the assault to break through German defences between the villages of Flers and Courcelette. Both were well behind German lines at the start of the battle, but a thrust between them parallel with the Roman road meant that a full cavalry corps could seize Bapaume. Once this position well to the rear of the existing German positions was in British hands, it was theoretically possible for the most mobile troops, the cavalry, to exploit the lack of German defences to 'roll up' the enemy position, pushing towards Arras. German troops in entrenched positions facing west would find British troops behind them and have no choice but to retreat or surrender. It was hoped that this bold move would unlock the trench stalemate and end the war in weeks or months. Once again, the prospect of such a complex operation with objectives well behind the existing frontline did not match Rawlinson's assessment of the ability of the troops under his command. He preferred the 'bite and hold' policy he had advocated on the first day and found himself being pushed by his Commander-in-Chief to be less cautious. Rawlinson was aware that his resources were limited and although the weight of shells fired by British artillery was heavier than on 1 July, it did not match that of 14 July.

HE LIED ABOUT HIS AGE

Buried in Dartmoor Cemetery in Bécourt on the Somme is Lieutenant Harry Webber. He was transport officer of 7th Battalion South Lancashire Regiment and died of wounds on 21 July 1916. At the time of his death, he was at least 67 years old.

To Blighty and home? British and German walking wounded escorted by a stretcher bearer with S.B. arm band head to the rear. Bernafay Wood, 19 July 1916. Note that the men's wounds have been bandaged. Some of them have been issued with an RAMC label to indicate the nature of their wounds and the treatment received to doctors further down the chain of evacuation.

In the battle that followed, the right-hand, southern XIV Corps was hampered by inadequate artillery preparation and the fact that a German strongpoint lay in one of the unshelled 'tank lanes'. Worse still, of the fifteen tanks allocated only two went into action. The result was that the 56th, 6th and Guards Divisions made little headway and took heavy casualties. The Guards did best, advancing 1,500yd, though they ended the day well short of their objective, Lesbœufs. The Guards' experience was matched by 14th (Light) Division of XV Corps, but to their north the newly arrived 41st Division achieved a spectacular success. By 8.30 a.m. tanks were seen in the village of Flers, the divisional objective, and within fifteen minutes infantry had joined them and occupied the north and west of the village. The area between Delville and High Woods was allotted to New Zealand Division, whose advance demonstrated a lack of experience of conditions on the Western Front. The division had previously served at Gallipoli and had a good reputation. On 15 September they were hampered by the late arrival of their supporting tanks and by their own errors. Twice during the day advancing New Zealand troops suffered casualties from their own supporting bombardment.

UNITED IN DEATH

In the same cemetery at Bécourt are the graves of gunners George and Robert Lee. They were father and son and were killed by the same shell on 5 September 1916.

However, by evening they had made contact with the men of 41st Division in Flers. XV Corps can be said to have done a good job. Sadly the same cannot be said of 47th Division on the flank of New Zealand Division. Their task was to capture High Wood, which had been attacked on so many previous occasions without success. The commander of III Corps felt that the wood could be secured with tanks, despite warnings from members of the fledgling Tank Corps that the vehicles were unsuitable for broken terrain littered with projecting branches and tree stumps. Lieutenant General Pulteney was insistent that tanks and not artillery would fire the infantry onto their first objective. The result was almost inevitable: only one tank was able to get into the wood and infantry casualties were high. The division captured the wood, but could not advance any further that day. To the north of this attack, despite being hampered by the failure to seize High Wood, 50th (Northumbrian) and 15th (Scottish) Divisions were able to capture the village of Martinpuich. On the front of the Reserve Army the Canadian Corps committed two divisions to the attack down the axis of the Albert–Bapaume road. On the left 2nd Canadian Division captured the village of Courcelette and on the north boundary of the battle 3rd Canadian Division took some sections of the key Fabeck Graben. Despite heavy and effective artillery support, both divisions were involved in fierce fighting with the German defenders and were unable to exploit their victories. By the end of the day the German third-line defences had been captured on a front of 4,500yd and to a depth of 2,500yd. Casualties were far fewer than 1 July, roughly half, and the ground captured double, but it was not the anticipated breakthrough. To make matters worse for the Allies, the French attack on the southern flank failed. It was a day of mistakes and over-ambition compounded by mechanical problems with the tanks, a failure to understand their limitations and a clear lack of training and experience. The German army were taken by surprise by the tanks, but had fought back and the tanks were destroyed by artillery fire and damaged or destroyed by armour-piercing bullets fired from rifles and machine guns. The Germans would soon develop anti-tank weapons and anticipated tactical success against this new weapon in future. There was no question of the Allies consolidating gains and going 'firm' on the line held on the evening of 15 September. The expectation of General Foch was that the battle would continue.

The continuation of the battle called for the capture of Morval on the boundary between the French and British armies. The French insisted on a daylight attack. As the tanks could not be hidden and used with the element of surprise Rawlinson held them in reserve; there were thus no restrictive 'tank lanes' and the barrage was able to cover the entire front of the advance. Other benefits for the British included a heavier concentration of artillery than ever before and weakness of the German positions. The battle commenced at 12.35 p.m. on 25 September and the infantry moved off close to a heavy creeping barrage, taking some casualties from their own guns, but confident that the Germans would be suppressed by the curtain of shells until they closed on their positions. The two corps involved, XIV and XV, were successful and the haul of prisoners high. In the southern sector 5th Division and the Guards from XIV captured Morval and Lesbœufs; to their north XV Corps' gains were initially not so great. However, it was discovered that the village of Gueudecourt, which had been heavily defended on the 25th, was evacuated by its defenders on the 26th. A similar situation pertained at Combles and the village was captured by units of 56th (London) Division and the linking French 6th Army.

The good news from the southern front was followed by similar reports from the Reserve Army in the north. General Gough launched the Battle of Thiepval Ridge on 26 September whose key success was the capture of the dominating Thiepval Chateâu and village positions by 18th Division. This division already had an excellent reputation and Major General Ivor Maxse had proved to be a brilliant leader. His planning was thorough and the division captured a position that most thought impregnable on the first day. Clearing the entire position took longer. German resistance at Mouquet Farm and elsewhere on the ridge was determined and the battle continued until the 28th. The Reserve Army, which became 5th Army at the end of October, was thus committed to a series of operations conducted by the Canadians close to Courcelette, which they had captured in September, and by British divisions to their north. These operations were collectively termed the Battle for the Ancre Heights as the ridge overlooked this tributary of the River Somme, which runs north to south across the region.

One reason for the Germans' stiff resistance in most areas was the fact that they knew that new lines of defence were being prepared to their rear. This offered the defenders the opportunity to fall back to successive prepared lines of defence, which now extended to the east of Bapaume. This construction took time and the Allies could, in theory, sweep over them with ease if they attacked before they

A British NCO looks at German dead at Guillemont near the remains of a flimsy shelter smashed by shellfire. The bodies are already attracting flies. They appear to have been searched and may well have been looted of their valuables.

Gunners manoeuvre a 60-pounder into position during the battle for Transloy Ridge in October 1916. Note the number of men required to move a single weapon and the increasing problem of mud. This weapon had a range of around 6.99 miles.

were complete. With this in mind, General Haig formulated a plan which called for a series of set-piece battles in which 3rd Army under Allenby would come into action near Gommecourt, 5th Army would attack on its current front and 4th Army would carry the Transloy Line prior to exploitation as far as Cambrai. Unfortunately, these actions coincided with a change in the weather and, after some success on the fronts of XV and III Corps, rain turned the battlefield into mud. Rain also reduced the effectiveness of forward observation officers of the artillery and prevented effective aerial observation because aircraft could not fly. Despite these handicaps, Rawlinson's men attempted to take positions on either side of the Bapaume road in worsening conditions. Not only did the battlefield turn into a quagmire, so did the roads to the rear and it became increasingly difficult to supply ammunition, rations and fodder for transport horses. In these circumstances, mud was an enemy second only to the Germans. By late October operations were restricted to single divisions at a time and by early November even senior officers were protesting to Rawlinson about the futile nature of such operations.

The remains of the village of Flers after the battle of mid-September. Some of the French inhabitants returned and commenced farming in early 1917. A year later, they were forced to flee their homes a second time in the German offensive of March 1918.

Men of the Border Regiment in 'Funk Holes' carved out of the side of a chalk trench in Thiepval Wood. These caves offered protection from enemy fire and the elements, but could be death traps in heavy shelling.

Though popular belief has it that Haig was ignorant or unconcerned about the realities of the frontline, it is clear that he was torn between the pressure to conclude operations for winter and complying with pressure from the French to do more. He was well aware that the 'wearing out fight' to which he had committed Rawlinson's army was a double-edged sword eroding his troops' ability to conduct this and future operations. To make matters worse, although General Foch was pressuring Haig to work alongside the French 6th Army in maintaining pressure on the German defences, he declined to provide the necessary support to do so. Central in the thrust towards Bapaume was the long operation to seize a Neolithic barrow at the Butte de Warlencourt. Shelling stripped the vegetation away from the mound and the gleaming white artificial chalk hill honeycombed with tunnels built by the German defenders withstood assault after assault form early October. It was still in German hands when the campaign concluded in November. But one final act remained to be played out before the campaign on the Somme ended.

The final operation was in the area that had witnessed the bloody defeat of 31st, 4th and 29th Divisions on the first day of battle. General Gough was instructed to prepare for a final effort to seize the ground north of the Ancre. Here the road network had survived better than the area to the south, which had been cut up by the constant movement of horses and motor vehicles required to supply 4th Army's operations. With flank support provided by XIII Corps, V Corps was intended to capture Beaumont-Hamel and Beaucourt while II Corps carried the area from Saint-Pierre-Divion and the Schwaben Redoubt. All these positions had resisted the attack of 1 July and the defenders were both confident and, if anything, better dug-in than previously. Delays caused by the weather put the operation back until 13 November. Preparations were careful and included a deception plan in which British artillery carried out pre-dawn bombardment to trick the defenders into expecting a regular and familiar pattern. The tunnel first used on 1 July to blow the crater under Hawthorn Redoubt was reopened. The main tunnel had been blocked with sand bags of spoil to prevent the original mine from blowing back, so the gallery was intact. A side tunnel was opened by Royal Engineers and, unknown to the German defenders who had used the existing crater as protection and had excavated new dugouts into its western face, a new 30,000lb mine was prepared. When this was blown it would entomb hundreds of defenders in their own underground workings. The plan for the attack on Beaumont-Hamel also included the extensive use of gas delivered by Livens Projectors. These could create such a heavy volume of gas that it would overcome German respirators and even kill men behind gas curtains in dugouts. As a final measure, the tanks were employed. The morning of 13 November was cold and foggy with limited visibility. This protected the British advance and limited German observation. Planning, weather and the combination of weapons favoured the attack.

The flank attacks of V Corps in the north carried out by 3rd and 31st Divisions were unsuccessful. The attack on Serre, the same objective given to 31st Division on 1 July, stalled. To their south, 2nd Division did better assisted greatly by the success of 51st (Highland) Division in their attack on the village of

Beaumont-Hamel and the Y-Ravine feature, which had been so dominant on the first day of battle. With tank, machine gun and heavy artillery support, the Highlanders succeeded in capturing the village, a regimental headquarters and the entire ravine. Germans gassed by the Livens projectiles littered the position and dugouts set on fire by British troops, to prevent the occupants appearing behind the first waves as they had on 1 July, burned for days as funeral pyres to their occupants. As if this were not success enough, 63rd (Royal Naval) Division captured Beaucourt on the banks of the River Ancre and advanced along the river valley to the east. As they did so, 39th and 19th Divisions of II Corps captured their objectives south of the river. The German front had seen positions taken, but the remaining troops fought on tenaciously and there was no general collapse. One example of this ability to endure the worst that the British could throw at them was the dogged defence of Redan Ridge. The operations of 4th Army finally ended on 18 November shortly after those of the French 6th Army the previous day and the last actions of Rawlinson's army on the 16th. This final small-scale but bitter action can be said to conclude the Battle of the Somme.

AFTER THE BATTLE

In simple terms, the result of the Battle of the Somme was that by mid-November 1916 the British army had advanced 7 miles, at the deepest point, into ground that had previously been held by German troops. This had been achieved at the cost of hundreds of thousands of British casualties, not to mention those of her French ally, and in purely cumulative terms those of the German army. The debate continues as to the exact numbers involved and recent estimates indicate that roughly 419,654 British soldiers were killed, wounded, missing or captured during the campaign, whilst French losses numbered 204,253. This gives a total of 623,907 for the Allied armies for a period of four and a half months of fighting on the Somme alone. This can be calculated as a daily loss of roughly 4,500 men. German casualties have previously been overestimated, but are now calculated to have been approximately 600,000, compared to 370,000 at Verdun. This means that, allowing for other losses during the year, the German army lost around 1 million soldiers during 1916. Admittedly, many of the wounded would recover and return to active service, but the implication for the German high command was clear. Unlike the British, they could not draw on the recruits of Kitchener's New Armies and certainly could not rely on the massive resources of the British Empire. By 1916 Canadian, Australian, New Zealand, South African and other troops had joined the existing British and Indian troops of the BEF on the Western Front. However, by this time troops from India, Africa and elsewhere in the British Empire were playing major roles in the campaigns of the Middle and Far East and Africa in what was increasingly a global struggle. Combined with conscription, which had come into force in most of the United Kingdom in January 1916, this meant that Britain's manpower was increasing rather than decreasing by the end of the year. The situation for the German army could not have been more different, and losses on the scale of Verdun and the Somme were unsustainable. The German Imperial Army was facing a manpower crisis. It was in recognition of this situation that German offensive operations were suspended at Verdun in mid-July and, later in the year, it was decided to withdraw to the *Siegfried Stellung* or 'Hindenburg Line'. This new defensive line was 25 miles behind the Somme and its construction was intended to allow the German army to withdraw to a prepared and advantageous position, consequently shortening its front with the Allies. This would offer considerable savings in manpower, but also reflected the German high command's doubt of its ability to resist a second Somme in 1917. In withdrawing to this position in late winter and early spring of 1917, the German army gave up

A chaplain tends a grave marked by a cross and helmet. The number of burials in this cemetery hint at the loss of life that resulted from the 'Big Push'. (IWM Q4004)

the position on the Somme it had so bitterly contested during the summer and autumn of the previous year.

As reports of the Somme offensive reached General Falkenhayn, he realised that his somewhat low opinion of the British and his confidence in the German 2nd Army's capacity to resist an Allied offensive on the Somme were misplaced. German units were largely too thinly spread to hold the ground they were allotted. Although some had successfully resisted attack on 1 July, others had crumbled. By 2 July, 2nd Army was waiting for the arrival of seven reinforcing divisions and a further seven within the week. They would be joined by a further twenty-eight divisions by the end of August. Most of these units went into the line facing Rawlinson's 4th and Gough's Reserve armies. The decision to suspend major offensive action at Verdun was a direct consequence of this leaching of German manpower to the Somme.

Whatever impact the Battle of the Somme ultimately had on future German strategy, the casualties of the first day that had the greatest impact on British public opinion at the time and subsequently. Unlike France or Germany, Britain had never before fielded an army that numbered in millions. The British public and politicians had no concept of the consequences of committing a large field army to a major battle. Even if successful, combat would result in mass casualties unprecedented for Britain. Before the 'Big Push', there was no public speculation about potential British casualties. Even though General Haig and his subordinates had calculated figures in the region of 40,000 killed and wounded, this did nothing to prepare people at home for the real figures. The casualty figures dwarfed those of earlier campaigns and many reacted with horror to the cost of war. Some politicians considered the losses unacceptable and spoke of a negotiated compromise peace. For individuals and communities, the flood of news that reached homes all over the United Kingdom was overwhelming and the outpouring of individual and collective grief was a shock to the nation. Nevertheless, although some individuals and groups felt that the human cost was too great, the vast majority of the population were brought together by the news of the casualties. Improvised shrines were established in some places and some sought comfort in their religious faith. People were not deterred from supporting the campaign and many felt that those who had already been killed would have died in vain unless the war was brought to a victorious conclusion. It is worth saying that public and military opinion in France concerning British casualties on the Somme was quite different. France was all too familiar with mass casualties of war. The more than 70,000 killed, wounded and captured on both sides at Borodino during Napoleon's invasion of Russia in 1812 were dwarfed by the nearly 1 million men lost by France in the Great War between its outbreak and the start of 1916. France expected heavy casualties in mass conscript armies. British losses at Neuve-Chapelle (12,000 killed or wounded) are put into the perspective of French opinion by their losses of 240,000 in the Battle of the Champagne – one of a series of costly attacks engaged in by their forces in the same year. If British casualties on the Somme were not comparable to the French, the latter were at least able to comment that Britain was, for the first time, 'playing its part' in the conflict. In a war of attrition, Britain's ally expected to see her take losses that reflected a proportionate contribution to the conflict. If this resulted in the death of British or imperial troops, public opinion on the Paris omnibus welcomed the obvious result that fewer French soldiers were dying.

News from the Eastern Front was good. The Somme offensive was part of a world strategy in which other members of the Entente played a part. Even before the Somme began, General Brusilov had mounted an offensive in the Carpathians. Facing troops that were not of the quality of the Western Front, with fewer guns and resources, the Russian forces broke the enemy lines in two places on a 300-mile front. This spectacular success forced the German army to send five much-needed divisions from the Western Front to Galicia to bolster her troops in the east. Lord Kitchener died en route to Russia. His role there was another means of demonstrating that Britain was playing a major role in the increasingly global Great War.

In August 1916, the seventy-minute documentary *The Battle of the Somme*, which had been filmed by cinematographers appointed by the War Office, was released. This remarkable documentary was seen by a third of Britain's population within months. Later

Unsere „Barbaren" im Feindesland

Dem Andenken des gefallenen Kameraden

German causalities mounted as the Somme battle dragged on into the autumn; here infantrymen remember a fallen comrade. By November, there were hundreds of thousands of such 'gefallenen'. (Author's collection) it was sent round the world to be seen on battlefields, in various parts of the Empire and world capitals. Despite the film's shocking nature, showing both German and British dead, this portrayal of the human cost of war was to help support the war effort rather than undermine it. The German response to the overwhelming success of *The Battle of the Somme* was to commission their own documentary *Heroes on the Somme*, though it did not receive quite the same response from the public. One enduring myth of the war comes from perhaps the most iconic sequence from *The Battle of the Somme*. This shows the explosion of the mine under Hawthorn Redoubt at Beaumont-Hamel. Malins filmed this famous scene at 7.20 a.m. on 1 July and went on to film British soldiers going into attack, running not walking, some of them falling under German fire. It was all filmed in long shot, however, and lacked detail and filmic 'impact'. In the period after the first day of battle, Malins took the opportunity to film men at the Trench Mortar Training School at Saint-Pol, well behind the lines. The two segments of film in which British soldiers climb out of shallow trenches to thread their way through barbed wire and disappear into smoke as some of their number 'die' are well known. They are used in virtually every documentary film about the Western Front and the Somme. Stills from the film feature in a multitude of books, particularly school textbooks, and have shaped our view of the war. The fact that the images, moving or still, are 'fake' is rarely challenged and they will doubtless be used again in the centenary years as 'evidence' of futile tactics and military incompetence. Of the entire film, which runs at over an hour, no more than a minute of the footage is faked. However, the faked sequence is so dramatic and so exactly matches what we think the Somme must have looked liked that it 'must' be used to support our preconceived ideas.

Among the casualties on the Somme were the men of the Pals battalions, who had flocked to the colours in 1914 and whose loss had notable local impact at home. These units largely recruited from the populous industrial cities and counties of northern England, drawing on men from urban communities, factories and other work places and even sports teams and clubs. The men had been motivated by a combination of patriotism and local pride. They joined up together, trained with work colleagues and neighbours and then went into battle with the same Pals. Although regular and territorial units had regional or county affiliations, their recruitment pattern meant that men from the same district or street rarely served in the same battalion. This was not the case with the Pals, many of whom had grown up together, attended the same schools or went to local clubs and pubs together. In terms of local pride and mutual support, this was a great strength, but also represented a fatal weakness. In the conditions of the Somme, where some units were held in reserve and others went into disastrous assaults, casualties varied widely. While some units lost few or even no men, others lost up to 80 per cent of their strength in hours or even minutes. In these circumstances, when a Pals unit suffered heavy losses the news could arrive in one part of a city that tens or hundreds of local men had been killed or wounded, while another area of the same community was spared. The most obvious example of this was the Accrington Pals, who served in 31st Division at Serre on 1 July. Their losses amounted to 584 men. This is not the highest loss of any British unit on that day, but resulted in the comment that the Pals had been 'Two years in the making. Ten minutes in the destroying'. It is, however, worth noting that this was written in 1961, not 1916.

In many ways, the modern view of the Somme took shape in the 1960s and later. The play *Oh, What a Lovely War!*, first produced in 1963, and then turned into a feature film in 1969, portrayed the war as futile and the generals as incompetent. The politician and author Alan Clark took the same approach in his highly critical book *The Donkeys* in 1961. In his thesis, the generals were culpable for the losses of the Western Front and effectively sacrificed the 'Lions' of the other ranks in their incompetence. In his popular history of

DUST NOT MUD TO START WITH

'As muddy as the Somme' is an often used term. However, the battle started on a hot, dry day and at times the problem was a shortage of water for men and animals. The mud came later.

the Great War, television historian A.J.P. Taylor describes the Western Front as 'A festival of mud and blood in which Generals blundered and politicians dithered'. The 1964 television series *The Great War* was rather more balanced. The fact that Basil Liddell Hart – one of the key historians contributing to the series, who was advisor for *Oh, What a Lovely War!* – refused to have his name linked to a balanced episode on the Battle of the Somme can be seen as evidence that this small group of influential people did much to create many of the enduring myths of the war and this battle specifically. More recently, the popular and entertaining television comedy series *Blackadder Goes Forth* took a similar stance on the incompetence of generals and the sacrificial role of junior officers and other ranks. In the final scene in the series the more sympathetic characters fall in an 'over the top' sequence which is doomed to failure in the face of enemy machine guns.

THE LEGACY

Ours is a generation that has seen the passing of the last of the veterans of the Great War. No more old soldiers will visit the scenes of their exploits on the Somme and their stories, if they are remembered, are the subject of family history and mythology. A fortunate few wrote memoirs or had biographies tying them to the Somme battlefield, but for the majority a name on a memorial or a fading postcard are all that is left to link people to this place. Despite this, the Somme exercises a remarkable and enduring power over later generations. In 2006 tens of thousands of visitors from all over Europe, not just Britain, made a pilgrimage to the Somme for the ninetieth anniversary events held at Beaumont-Hamel, the Ulster Tower, Thiepval and Lochnagar Crater. However, there is no question that the scale of the events on the Somme in 2016 will surpass those of previous generations. In the immediate post-war world thousands of veterans and their families arrived by train or bus to see the beautiful newly opened cemeteries built by the Imperial War Graves Commission or to look for names on the monument to the missing at Thiepval, those of friends and comrades. That generation may even have personally seen the 'missing' die on the battlefield and regretted their inability to give their 'pals' a decent grave. Yet they went back and so have subsequent generations keen to walk the battlefield and hunt for souvenirs of the fighting or evidence of the events that occurred on this patch of French farmland.

A 9.2in Howitzer in a firing position in Carnoy Valley in September 1916. This weapon could fire a 290lb shell 7.9 miles.

The cost of war. Stretcher bearers move over open ground in daylight to rescue a wounded comrade. Note the steel sniper plates and stick grenades in the damaged German position to their left.

So why was the ninetieth anniversary event of 2006 so large? Why will the centenary event of 2016 be even bigger than anything seen previously? The answer is the ability of the name of the Battle of the Somme to evoke such strong emotions in generations that have no direct contact with the events of 1916 or later in the war. The Somme is studied in schools, is the subject of thousands of battlefield coach trips every year, and it is possible to find British registered cars turning round in muddy gateways almost every day of the year. Documentary films, dramas, computer games and internet forums have fuelled this interest. Virtually everyone in the western world knows something about the Somme and they have strong opinions about how the battle was fought, the losses on both sides and what the area means to them. The Ypres Salient is demonstrably more frequently visited than the Somme and has the advantage of the daily ceremony of the Last Post at the Menin Gate, which provides a focus for the day's visitors.

However, despite the tens of thousands of names of the missing on the Menin Gate, and thousands more at Tyne Cot, the Salient does not quite conjure such strong opinions as the Somme. Even today, people describe bad weather as being 'As muddy as the Somme'. British Second World War soldiers serving in Burma, a world away from the chalk downs of northern France, described every operation that went wrong as being 'The biggest balls-up since the Somme'. The Battle of the Somme has become the epitome of the Great War, as it is popularly seen. Futile, muddy, bloody and unnecessary. The ultimate expression of this can be seen in the attitude towards a single day in the four-month battle. The date 1 July remains the focus of attention and commemoration. Hundreds, if not thousands, of visitors arrive before 7.30 a.m. at multiple events held every 1 July at Beaumont-Hamel, the Ulster Tower and Lochnagar Crater. In 2006, whilst waiting for the ceremony at the Lochnagar Crater to begin, the then Director of the *Historial de la Grande Guerre* in Péronne, Guillaume de Fonclare, said to me, 'You British are odd.' I asked why. His reply was that it struck him that we, the British, liked failure. He pointed out that all the ceremonies held that morning marked places at which the attack failed at least partly. His question was why did no one ever 'have a cup of tea in Montauban' in the late afternoon to celebrate, rather than commemorate, the capture of that village late in the afternoon of 1 July 1916?

The answer has to be that those people who attend the events on 1 July have a singularly myopic view of the day. By concentrating on tragedy, they can effectively ignore the triumphs of the same day. Essentially, the events of 1 July can be seen as a self-fulfilling prophecy. Everyone knows that the day was a disaster and by returning to the places on which this situation was so marked visitors can reassure themselves that the battle had no redeeming features. In this interpretation, those men who were wounded or lost their lives on the first day of the Somme were 'wasted', their deaths were 'futile'. To make this worse, if this were possible, the decision taken by the generals, specifically Haig, to continue the battle through subsequent weeks and months 'proves' their culpability in the 'useless slaughter of a generation'. Relatively few Somme battlefield tourists find time to visit locations linked with the continuing battle

An 8in MkV Howitzer at the moment of firing in wet conditions, in Aveluy, September 1916. Note the use of woodland as camouflage from enemy observation. This weapon could fire a 200lb shell about 6.2 miles.

of 1916. It is fair to say that hundreds of thousands visit the memorial to the missing at Thiepval every year, but not to recall the brilliant capture of this formidable position by 18th Division in September 1916. The little monument to the men who captured this strongpoint that had resisted all attacks since July goes largely unnoticed. The same can be said for the sites at Delville Wood and Pozières, which are now associated with the South Africans and Australians. The role of these divisions in the successful battle of late July and August is possibly obscured by the national memorial to the South Africans at Delville and the profusion of flagstaffs, cafes and other monuments in Pozières. An exception is the monument to 38th (Welsh Division) at Memetz. This isolated and quite modern monument, almost an afterthought compared with many others, ties Lloyd George's Welsh Army into the landscape of the 'battle for the woods'. Sadly, it has relatively few visitors. Elsewhere, with few monuments and little information for visitors, most of the other locations on the Somme remain obscure if not forgotten. Because of this, the number of people who attend the simple ceremony held at the flagstaff in Beaumont-Hamel on 13 November every year, which marks the capture of the village in November 1916, can be counted on the fingers of two hands. Many of these are local villagers rather than battlefield tourists.

This situation perfectly mirrors popular opinion of the battle. We recall in vast detail the first day, have a vague knowledge of the events of August into September, but no interest in the culmination of the campaign in mid-November. The muddy final days of the Somme are seen as an unnecessary prolongation of an unnecessary battle in which hundreds of thousands of lives were wasted by the generals. This interpretation requires the believers to have no knowledge of, or interest in, the military and political background to the battle. To disregard the international imperative to demonstrate Britain's ability to play a major part in the war and support her French ally. Further, it requires a wilful disregard of the way in which the battle developed, how it put pressure on the German army, specifically as irreplaceable German casualties mounted. It led to the collapse of the German offensive at Verdun and, ultimately, to the withdrawal of their forces from the Somme.

One commentator claimed that the Battle of the Somme was futile, even unnecessary, because the German army withdrew to their prepared defences in the spring of 1917. The fact that this would not have happened without the battle does not matter to those who seek to blame individuals or organisations for historical events. Hundreds of thousands of words have been used to explain events such as Pearl Harbour in December 1941, the attack on the Twin Towers in New York in 2001. Straightforward explanations are rejected and replaced by international conspiracies in which shadowy forces intrigue to bring the USA into the Second World War, the CIA rather than suicide pilots blow up the Twin Towers. These conspiracy theories reject rational explanation in exchange for complex webs involving international politicians, shadowy and manipulative corporations and secret societies. This process of rewriting history has been described as revisionism and is a well-recognised feature of historical study and debate. It is therefore worthy of note that historians who had explained the need to fight the Battle of the Somme in terms some would argue to be sympathetic to the generals involved, or who have justified the casualties as unfortunate but necessary, have been labelled 'revisionists'. The fact that many of those involved in this process of so-called 'revisionism' are highly qualified academics, rather than homespun conspiracy theorists, does not, it would appear, matter.

Professor Gary Sheffield, who, as part of a television documentary, explained the gradual tactical improvement of the British army during the continuing Somme battle, was accused of being part of a militaristic 'cover-up' of the facts. Essentially, some people, despite careful historical arguments and explanations, simply want the Somme to be futile because it fits their personal and sometimes, collective, conclusion. The fact that the area of the Somme over which the battle was fought in 1916 was the site of a highly success British campaign in the summer of 1918 is little known. If people realised this, their understanding of the Great War and specifically the development of the British army, its tactics and methods of warfare might be changed.

Following the faltering steps of 1916 with the first use of artillery barrages, co-operation with aircraft, the use of armoured vehicles and improved small-unit tactics in an 'all arms' battle, all of which were outcomes of if not born on the Somme, the British army that attacked German positions on the Somme in August and September 1918 was a 'war winning' force composed of officers and men who had learned from the mistakes made on the same ground two years earlier. Professor Peter Simkins has demonstrated that positions on the Somme which held out for weeks or months in 1916 fell in hours or days to this New Army. The reason for these rapid victories was not the collapse of the German army; that would follow later in the '100 Days' which took the Allies to the line reached on 11 November 1918. Rather, it was the use of new tactics, intelligent and well-trained troops and experienced and able officers, most of whom had been part of the 1916 battle. The culmination of Professor Sheffield's 'learning Loch Ness Monster' can be seen in these swift victories, rapid advances and the liberation of French soil. Sadly, these victories did not come cheaply and the casualties of 1918 were higher on a day-to-day basis than those of 1916. The difference is that the men who fell on the Somme in 1918 were on their way to victory, but unlike their comrades of 1916, are largely forgotten. It would appear that we have developed a broad opinion of the Great War in which soldiers in the British army are collectively 'victims', not 'victors'.

There is no question that the Battle of the Somme will continue to polarise opinion into the twenty-first century. Future generations will endlessly debate the rights and wrongs of the campaign and war in general. However, I would prefer to trust to a man who was there to provide an opinion for those in subsequent generations with the marvellous benefit of hindsight. For this reason I rely on my grandfather, a man who served as a private soldier on the Somme, and then right through to the end of the war. Despite being wounded twice and gassed once by the enemy, he stood by both the generals and his comrades. 'The generals did their job. We did ours. We won!' he said. The military of the Great War cannot be blamed for the failure to capitalise on the peace that the British army and its allies achieved. It was a collective political failure that led to the outbreak of the Second World War and it was left to the children of the Great War generation to bring that second world conflict to a successful conclusion. If that second war made the first 'futile', it is only with the knowledge of events after the armistice of 11 November 1918 that this judgement can be made. Someone once said that 'fighting for peace is like fornicating for virginity'. As events have shown, two world wars and the threat of nuclear Armageddon have not stopped politicians from sending soldiers to try.

ORDERS OF BATTLE

British Expeditionary Force: General Sir Douglas Haig

Fourth Army: General Sir Henry Rawlinson
Reserve/Fifth Army: General Sir Hubert Gough
Third Army: General Sir E. Allenby
II Corps: Lieutenant General C.W. Jacob
III Corps: Lieutenant General Sir W.P. Pulteney
V Corps: Lieutenant General E.A. Fanshawe
VII Corps: Lieutenant General Sir T.D'O. Snow
VIII Corps: Lieutenant General Sir A.G. Hunter-Weston
X Corps: Lieutenant General Sir T.L.N. Morland
XIII Corps: Lieutenant General Sir W.N. Congreve
XIV Corps: Lieutenant General the Earl of Cavan
XV Corps: Lieutenant General H.S. Horne (later commanded
    1st Army) replaced by Lieutenant General J.P. Du Cane
1 Anzac: Lieutenant General Sir W.R. Birdwood
Canadian Corps: Lieutenant General The Hon. Sir J. Byng

Guards Division: Major General G.P.T. Fielding

1st Guards Brigade
2/Grenadier Guards
2/Coldstream Guards
3/Coldstream Guards
1/Irish Guards

2nd Guards Brigade
3/Grenadier Guards
1/Coldstream Guards
1/Scots Guards
2/Irish Guards

3rd Guards Brigade
1/Grenadier Guards
4/Grenadier Guards
2/Scots Guards
1/Welsh Guards

Pioneers
4/Coldstream Guards

1st Division: Major General E.P. Strickland

1st Brigade
10/Glosters
1/ Black Watch
8/R. Berkshires
1/Camerons

2nd Brigade
2/R. Sussex
1/Loyal North Lancashires

1/Northamptons
2/King's Royal Rifle Corps

3rd Brigade
1/South Wales Borderers
1/Glosters
2/Welsh
2/R. Munster Fus.

Pioneers
1/6th Welsh

2nd Division: Major General W.G. Walker

5th Brigade
17/R. Fus.
24/R. Fus.
2/Ox and Bucks Light Infantry (LI)
2/Highland LI

6th Brigade
1/King's Regt
2/S. Staffordshires
13/Essex
17/Middlesex

99th Brigade
22/R. Fus.
23/R. Fus.
1/R. Berkshires
1/King's Royal Rifle Corps

Pioneers
10/Duke of Cornwall's LI

3rd Division: Major General J.A. Haldane
(Promoted to command
VI Corps then Major General
C.J. Deverell)

8th Brigade
2/R. Scots
8/E. Yorkshires
1/R. Fus.
7/King's Shropshire LI

9th Brigade
1/Northumberland Fus.
4/R. Fus.
13/King's Regt
12/W. Yorkshires

76th Brigade
8/King's Own (Royal Lancaster)
2/Suffolks
10/R. Welch
1/Gordons

Pioneers
20/King's Royal Rifle Corps

4th Division: Major General the Hon. W. Lambton

10th Brigade
1/R. Warwickshire
2/Seaforths
1/ R. Irish Fus.
2/R. Dublin Fus.

12th Brigade
1/King's Own (Royal Lancaster)
2/Lancashire Fus.
2/Duke of Wellington's
2/Essex

11th Brigade
1/Somerset LI
1/E. Lancashire
1/Hampshire
1/Rifle Brigade

Pioneers
21/W. Yorkshires

5th Division: Major General R.B. Stephens

13th Brigade
14/R. Warwicks
15/R. Warwicks
2/Kings Own Scottish Borderers
1/R. West Kent

15th Brigade
16/R. Warwicks
1/Norfolks
1/Bedfords
1/Cheshires

95th Brigade
1/Devonshire
12/Glosters
1/E. Surreys
1/Duke of Cornwall's LI

Pioneers
1/6 Argyll & Sutherland

6th Division: Major General C. Ross

16th Brigade
1/Buffs (East Kent)
8/Bedfords
1/King's Shropshire LI
2/York and Lancaster

18th Brigade
1/W. Yorkshires
11/Essex
2/Durham LI
14/Durham LI

71st Brigade
9/Norfolks
9/Suffolks
1/Leicesters
2/Sherwood Foresters

Pioneers
11/Leicesters

7th Division: Major General H.E. Watts

20th Brigade
8/Devonshire
9/Devonshire
2/Borders
2/Gordons

91st Brigade
2/Queen's
1/S. Staffordshires
21/Manchesters (Manchester Pals 6th)
22/Manchesters (Manchester Pals 7th)

22nd Brigade
2/R. Warwickshire
2/R. Irish
1/R. Welch Fus.
20/Manchesters (Manchester Pals 5th)

Pioneers
24/Manchesters (Oldham Pals)

8th Division: Major General H. Hudson

23rd Brigade
2/Devonshire
2/W. Yorkshires
2/Scottish Rifles
2/Middlesex

24th Brigade
1/Worcesters
1/Sherwood Foresters
2/Northamptons
2/E. Lancashires

25th Brigade
2/Lincolns
2/R. Berkshire
1/R. Irish Rifles
2/Rifle Brigade

Pioneers
22/Durham LI

9th (Scottish) Division: Major General W.T. Furse

26th Brigade
8/Black Watch
7/Seaforths
5/Camerons
10/Argyll & Sutherland

South African Brigade
1st Regt (Cape Province)
2nd Regt (Natal & O.F.S)
3rd Regt (Transvaal & Rhodesia)
4th Regt (Scottish)

27th Brigade
11/R. Scots
12/R. Scots
6/King's Own Scottish Borderers
9/Scottish Rifles

Pioneers
9/Seaforths

11th Division: Major General Sir C. Woollcombe

32nd Brigade
9/W. Yorkshires
6/Green Howards
8/Duke of Wellington's
6/York and Lancaster

33rd Brigade
6/Lincolns
6/Borders
7/S. Staffordshires
9/Sherwood Foresters

34th Brigade
8/Northumberland Fus.
9/Lancashire Fus.
5/Dorsets
11/Manchesters

Pioneers
6/E. Yorkshires

12th Division: Major General A.B. Scott

35th Brigade
7/Norfolks
7/Suffolks
9/Essex
5/R. Berkshires

36th Brigade
8/R. Fus.
9/R. Fus.
7/R. Sussex
11/Middlesex

37th Brigade
6/Queen's
6/Buffs
7/E. Surreys
6/R. West Kents

Pioneers
5/Northamptons

14th (Light) Division: Major General V.A. Couper

41st Brigade
7/King's Royal Rifle Corps
8/King's Royal Rifle Corps
7/Rifle Brigade
8/Rifle Brigade

42nd Brigade
5/Ox and Bucks LI
5/King's Shropshire LI
9/King's Royal Rifle Corps
9/Rifle Brigade

43rd Brigade
6/Somerset LI
6/Duke of Cornwall's LI
6/King's Own Yorkshire LI (KOYLI)
10/Durham LI

Pioneers
11/King's Regt

15th (Scottish) Division: Major General F.W.N. McCraken

44th Brigade
9/Black Watch
8/Seaforths
8/10 Gordons
7/Camerons

45th Brigade
13/R. Scots
6/7 R. Scots Fus.
6/Camerons
11/ Argyll & Sutherlands

46th Brigade
10/Scottish Rifles
7/8 King's Own Scottish Borderers
10/11 Highland LI
12/Highland LI

Pioneers
9/Gordons

16th (Irish) Division: Major General W.B. Hickie

47th Brigade
6/R. Irish
6/Connaught Rangers
7/Leinsters
8/R. Munster Fus.

48th Brigade
7/Irish Rifles
1/R. Munster Fus.
8/R. Dublin Fus.
9/R. Dublin Fus.

49th Brigade
7/R. Inniskilling Fus.
8/ R. Inniskilling Fus.
7/R. Irish Fus.
8/R. Irish Fus.

Pioneers
11/Hampshires

17th (Northern) Division: Major General T.D. Pilcher

50th Brigade
10/W. Yorkshires
7/E. Yorkshires
7/Green Howards
6/Dorsetshire

51st Brigade
7/Lincolns
7/Borders
8/S. Staffordshires
10/Sherwood Foresters

52nd Brigade
9/Northumberland Fus.
10/Lancashire Fus.
9/Duke of Wellington's
12/Manchesters

Pioneers
7/York & Lancaster

18th (Eastern) Division: Major General F.I. Maxse

53rd Brigade
8/Norfolk
8/Suffolk
10/Essex
6/R. Berkshire

54th Brigade
11/R. Fus.
7/Bedfordshire
6/Northamptonshire
12/Middlesex

55th Brigade
7/Queen's
7/Buffs.
8/E. Surrey
7/R. West Kent

Pioneers
8/R. Sussex

19th (Western) Division (New Army): Major General G.T.M. Bridges

56th Brigade
7/King's Own
7/E. Lancashire
7/S. Lancashire
7/Loyal North Lancashires

57th Brigade
10/R. Warwickshire
8/Gloucestershire
10/Worcestershire
8/N. Staffordshires

58th Brigade
9/Cheshire
9/R. Welch Fus.
9/Welch
6/Wiltshire

Pioneers
5/South Wales Borderers

20th (Light) Division: Major General W.D. Smith

59th Brigade
10/King's Royal Rifle Corps
11/King's Royal Rifle Corps
10/Rifle Brigade
11/Rifle Brigade

60th Brigade
6/Ox and Buck LI
6/King's Shropshire LI
12/King's Royal Rifle Corps
11/Rifle Brigade

61st Brigade
7/Somerset LI
7/Duke of Cornwall's LI
7/KOYLI
12/King's Regt

Pioneers
11/Durham LI

21st Division: Major General D.G.M. Campbell

62nd Brigade
12/Northumberland Fus.
13/Northumberland Fus.
1/Lincolns
10/Green Howards

63rd Brigade
8/Lincolns
8/Somerset LI
4/Middlesex
10/York & Lancaster

64th Brigade
1/E. Yorkshires
9/KOYLI
10/KOYLI
15/Durham LI

Pioneers
14/Northumberland Fus.

23rd Division: Major General J.M. Babington

68th Brigade
10/Northumberland Fus.
11/Northumberland Fus.
12/Durham LI
13/Durham LI

69th Brigade
11/W. Yorkshires
8/Green Howards
9/Green Howards
10/Duke of Wellington's

70th Brigade
11/Sherwood Foresters
8/KOYLI
8/York and Lancaster
9/York and Lancaster

Pioneers
9/S. Staffordshires

24th Division: Major General J.E. Capper

17th Brigade
8/Buffs
1/R. Fus.
12/R. Fus.
3/Rifle Brigade

72nd Brigade
8/Queen's
9/E. Surreys
8/R. West Kents
1/N. Staffordshires

73rd Brigade
9/R. Sussex
7/Northamptons
13/Middlesex
2/Leinsters

Pioneers
12/Sherwood Foresters

25th Division: Major General E.G.T Bainbridge

7th Brigade
10/Cheshires
3/Worcesters
8/Loyal North Lancashires
3/Rifle Brigade

74th Brigade
11/Lancashire Fus.
13/Cheshires
9/Loyal North Lancashires
1/N. Staffordshires

75th Brigade
11/Cheshires
8/Borders
2/South Lancashires
8/South Lancashires

Pioneers
6/South Wales Borderers

29th Division: Major General H. de B. de Lisle

86th Brigade
2/R. Fus.
1/Lancashire Fus.
16/Middlesex
1/R. Dublin Fus.

87th Brigade
2/South Wales Borderers
1/King's Own Scottish Borderers
1/R. Inniskilling Fus.
1/Borders

88th Brigade
4/Worcesterhire
2/Hampshire
1/Essex
Newfoundland Regt

Pioneers
1/2nd Monmouthshire

30th Division: Major General J.S.M. Shea

21st Brigade
18/King's
2/Green Howards
2/Wiltshire
19/Manchesters

89th Brigade
17/King's
19/King's
20/King's
2/Bedfords

90th Brigade
2/R. Scots Fus.
16/Manchesters
17/Manchesters
18/Manchesters

Pioneers
11/S. Lancashire

31st Division: Major General R. Wanless O'Gowan

92nd Brigade
10/E. Yorkshires (Hull Commercials)
11/E. Yorkshires (Hull tradesmen)
12/E. Yorkshires (Hull sportsmen)
12/E. Yorkshires (T'others)

94th Brigade
11/E. Lancashire (Accrington Pals)
12/York & Lancaster (Shefiield City Bn.)
13/York & Lancaster (Barnsley Pals, 1st)
14/York & Lancaster (Barnsley Pals, 2nd)

93rd Brigade
15/W. Yorkshires (Leeds Pals)
16/W. Yorkshires (Bradford Pals 1st)
18/W. Yorkshires (Bradford Pals 2nd)
18/Durham LI (Durham Pals)

Pioneers
12/K.O.Y. LI (Halifax Pals)

32nd Division: Major General W.H. Rycroft

14th Brigade
19/Lancashire Fus. (Salford Pals 3rd)
1/Dorsetshire
2/Manchesters
15/Highland LI (Glasgow Tramways)

96th Brigade
16/Northumberland Fus. (Newcastle Commercials)
15/Lancashire Fus. (Salford Pals 1st)
2/R. Inniskilling Fus.

97th Brigade
11/Borders (Lonsdales)
2/KOYLI
16/Highland LI (Glasgow Boys Brigade)
17/Highland LI (Glasgow Commercial)

Pioneers
17/Northumberland Fus. (Newcastle Railway Pals)
16/Lancashire Fus. (Salford Pals 2nd)

33rd Division: Major General H.J.S. Landon, then Major General R.J. Pinney

19th Brigade
20/R. Fus.
2/R. Welch Fus.
1/Camerons
5/Scottish Rifles

98th Brigade
4/King's
1/4 Suffolks
1/Middlesex
2/Argyll & Sutherland

100th Brigade
1/Queens
2/Worcesters
16/King's Royal Rifle Corps
1/9Highland LI

Pioneers
18/Middlesex

34th Division (New Army): Major General C. Ingouville-Williams (killed), then Major General C.L. Nicholson

101st Brigade
15/R. Scots (Edinburgh City 1st)
16/R. Scots Edinburgh City 2nd)
10/Lincolns (Grimsby Chums)
11/Suffolk

102nd Division
20/Northumberland Fus. (Tyneside Scottish 1st)
21/Northumberland Fus. (Tyneside Scottish 2nd)
22/Northumberland Fus. (Tyneside Scottish 3rd)
23/Northumberland Fus. (Tyneside Scottish 4th)

103rd (Tyneside Irish) Brigade
24/Northumberland Fus. (Tyneside Irish1st)
25/Northumberland Fus. (Tyneside Irish 2nd)
26/Northumberland Fus. (Tyneside Irish 3rd)
27/Northumberland Fus. (Tyneside Irish 4th)

Pioneers
18/Northumberland Fus.
(Tyneside Pioneers)

35th (Bantam) Division: Major General R.J. Pinney

104th Brigade
17/Lancashire Fus.
18/Lancashire Fus.
20/Lancashire Fus.
23/Manchesters

105th Brigade
15/Cheshires
16/Cheshires
14/Glosters
15/Sherwood Foresters

106th Brigade
17/R. Scots
17/W. Yorkshires
19/Durham LI
18/Highland LI

Pioneers
19/Northumberland Fus.

36th (Ulster) Division: Major General O.S.W. Nugent

107th Brigade
8/R. Irish Rifles (East Belfast)
9/R. Irish Rifles (West Belfast)
10/R. Irish Rifles (South Belfast)
15/R. Irish Rifles (North Belfast)

108th Brigade
11/R. Irish Rifles (South Antrim)
12/R. Irish Rifles (Central Antrim)
13/R. Irish Rifles (County Down)
9/R. Irish Fus. (Co. Armagh, Monaghan & Cavan)

109th Brigade
9/R. Inniskilling Fus. (County Tyrone)
10/R. Inniskilling Fus. (County Derry)
11/R. Inniskilling Fus. (Donegal & Fermanagh)
14/R. Irish Rifles (Belfast Young Citizens)

Pioneers
16/R. Irish Rifles (County Down 2nd)

37th Division: Major General Count Gleichen

110th Brigade
6/Leicestershire
7/Leicestershire
8/Leicestershire
9/Leicestershire

111th Brigade
10/R. Fus.
13/R. Fus.
13/King's Royal Rifle Corps
13/Rifle Brigade

112th Brigade
11/R. Warwickshire
6/Bedfordshire
8/E. Lancashire
10/Loyal North Lancashires

Pioneers
9/N. Staffordshires

38th (Welsh) Division: Major General I. Philipps (relieved), then Major General C.G. Blackader

113th Brigade
13/R. Welch Fus.
14/R. Welch Fus.
15/R. Welch Fus.
16/R. Welch Fus.

114th Brigade
10/Welch
13/Welch
14/Welch
15/Welch

115th Brigade
10/South Wales Borderers
11/South Wales Borderers
17/R. Welch Fus.
16/Welch

Pioneers
19/Welch

39th Division: Major General G.J. Cuthbert

116th Brigade
11/R. Sussex
12/R. Sussex
13/R. Sussex
14/Hampshires

117th Brigade
16/Sherwood Foresters
17/Sherwood Foresters
17/King's Royal Rifle Brigade
16/Rifle Brigade

118th Brigade
1/6 Cheshires
1/1 Cambridgeshires
1/1 Hertfordshires
4/5 Black Watch

Pioneers
13/Gloucesters

41st Division: Major General S.T.B. Lawford

122nd Brigade
12/E. Surreys
15/Hampshires
11/R. West Kents

123rd Brigade
11/Queen's
10/R. West Kents
20/Durham LI

124th Brigade
10/Queen's
26/R. Fus.
32/R. Fus.
21/King's Royal Rifle Corps

Pioneers
19/Middlesex

46th (North Midland) Division T.F.: Major General the Hon. E.J. Montagu-Stuart-Wortley

137th Brigade
1/5th S. Staffordshires
1/6th S. Staffordshires
1/5th N. Staffordshires
1/6th N. Staffordshires

138th Brigade
1/4 Lincolns
1/5 Lincolns
1/4 Leicestershire
1/5 Leicestershire

139th Brigade
1/5 Sherwood Foresters
1/6 Sherwood Foresters
1/7 Sherwood Foresters (Robin Hood Rifles)
1/8 Sherwood Foresters

Pioneers
1/1 Monmouthshire

47th (1/2 London) Division T.F.: Major General Sir C. St L. Barter (relieved), then Major General G.F. Gorringe

140th Brigade
1/6 Londons (City of London)
1/7 Londons (City of London
1/8 Londons (Post Office Rifles)
1/1 London (Civil Service Rifles)

141st Brigade
1/7 Londons (Poplar and Stepney Rifles)
1/18 Londons (London Irish Rifles)
1/19 Londons (St Pancras)
1/20 Londons (Blackheath and Woolwich)

142nd Brigade
1/21 Londons (1st Surrey Rifles)
1/22 Londons (The Queen's)
1/23 Londons
1/24 Londons (The Queen's)

Pioneers
1/4 R. Welch Fus.

48th (South Midland) Division T.F.: Major General R. Fanshawe

143rd Brigade
1/5 R. Warwickshire – attached to 4th Division 1/5 Gloucestershire

1/6 R. Warwickshire
1/7 R. Warwickshire
1/8 R. Warwickshire – attached
to 4th Division
1/4 R. Berkshire

145th Brigade
1/4 Oxf. & Bucks. LI
1/Bucks.

144th Brigade
1/4 Gloucestershire
1/6 Gloucestershire
1/7 Worcestershire
1/8 Worcestershire

Pioneers
1/5 R. Sussex

49th (West Riding) Division T.F.: Major General E.M. Perceval

146th Brigade
1/5 W. Yorkshires
1/6 W. Yorkshires
1/7 W. Yorkshires
1/8 W. Yorkshires

147th Brigade
1/4 Duke of Wellington's
1/5 Duke of Wellington's
1/6 Duke of Wellington's
1/7 Duke of Wellington's

148th Brigade
1/4 KOYLI
1/5 York & Lancaster
1/4 York & Lancaster
1/5 York & Lancaster

Pioneers
1/3 Monmouthshire

50th (Northumbrian) Division T.F.: Major General P.S. Wilkinson

149th Brigade
1/4 Northumberland Fus.
1/5 Northumberland Fus.
1/6 Northumberland Fus.
1/7 Northumberland Fus.

150th Brigade
1/4 E. Yorkshires
1/4 Green Howards
1/5 Green Howards
1/5 Durham LI

151st Brigade
1/5 Borders
1/6 Durham LI
1/8 Durham LI
1/9 Durham LI

Pioneers
1/7 Durham LI

51st (Highland) Division T.F.:
Major General G.M. Harper

152nd Brigade
1/5 Seaforths
1/6 Seaforths
1/6 Gordons
1/8 Argyll & Sutherland
Highlanders

153rd Brigade
1/6 Black Watch
1/7 Black Watch
1/5 Gordons
1/7 Gordons

154th Brigade
1/9 R. Scots
1/4 Seaforths
1/4 Gordons
1/7 Argyll & Sutherland
Highlanders

Pioneers
1/7 Durham LI

55th (West Lancashire)
Division T.F.: Major General
H.S. Jeudwine

164th Brigade
1/4 King's Own
1/8 King's
2/5 Lancashire Fus.
1/3 Loyal North Lancashires

165th Brigade
1/5 King's
1/6 King's
1/7 King's
1/9 King's

166th Brigade
1/5 King's Own
1/10 King's
1/5 South Lancashires
1/5 Loyal North Lancashires

Pioneers
1/4 South Lancashires

56th (1st London) Division
T.F.: Major General C.P.A.
Hull

167th Brigade
1/1st London
1/3rd London
1/7th Middlesex
1/8th Middlesex

168th Brigade
1/4th London
1/12th London (Rangers)
1/13th London (Kensington)
1/14th London (London Scottish)

169th Brigade
1/2nd London
1/5th London (London Rifle
Brigade)
1/9th London (Queen Victoria's
Rifles)

1/6th London (Queen's Westminster Rifles)

Pioneers
1/5th Cheshire

63rd (Royal Naval) Division: Major General Sir A. Paris (wounded), then Major General C.D. Shute

188th Brigade
Anson Battalion
Howe Battalion
1/R. Marine Battalion
2/R. Marine Battalion

189th Brigade
Hood Battalion
Nelson Battalion
Hawke Battalion
Drake Battalion

190th Brigade
1/Honourable Artillery Company
7/R. Fus.
4/Bedfords
10/R. Dublin Fus.

Pioneers
14/Worcestershires

1st Australian Division: Major General H.B. Walker

1st (New South Wales) Brigade

1st Battalion
2nd Battalion
3rd Battalion
4th Battalion

2nd (Victoria) Brigade
5th Battalion
6th Battalion
7th Battalion
8th Battalion

3rd Brigade
9th (Queensland) Battalion
10th (South Australia) Battalion
11th (West Australia) Battalion
12th (South and West Australia) Battalion

Pioneers
1st Australian Pioneer Battalion

2nd Australian Division: Major General J.G. Legge

5th (New South Wales) Brigade
17th Battalion
18th Battalion
19th Battalion
20th Battalion

6th (Victoria) Brigade
21st Battalion
22nd Battalion
23rd Battalion
24th Battalion

7th Brigade
25th (Queensland) Battalion
26th (Queensland, Tasmania) Battalion
27th (South Australia) Battalion
28th (West Australia) Battalion

Pioneers
2nd Australian Pioneer Battalion

4th Australian Division: Major General Sir H. Cox

4th Brigade
13th (New South Wales) Battalion
14th (Victoria) Battalion
15th (Queensland, Tasmania) Battalion
16th (South and West Australia) Battalion

12th Brigade
45th (New South Wales) Battalion
46th (Victoria) Battalion
47th (Queensland, Tasmania) Battalion
48th (South and West Australia) Battalion

13th Brigade
49th (Queensland) Battalion
50th (South Australia) Battalion
51st (West Australia) Battalion
52nd (South and West Australia) Battalion

Pioneers
4th Australian Pioneer Battalion

5th Australian Division: Major General the Hon. J.W. McCay

8th Brigade
29th (Victoria) Battalion
30th (New South Wales) Battalion
31st (Queensland and Victoria) Battalion
32nd (South and West Australia) Battalion

14th (New South Wales) Brigade
53rd Battalion
54th Battalion
55th Battalion
56th Battalion

15th (Victoria) Brigade
57th Battalion
58th Battalion
59th Battalion
60th Battalion

Pioneers
5th Australian Pioneer Battalion

1st Canadian Division: Major General A.W. Currie

1st Brigade
1st (Ontario) Battalion
2nd (East Toronto) Battalion

3rd Battalion (Toronto Regt)
4th Battalion

2nd Brigade

5th (Western Cavalry) Battalion
7th Battalion (1st British Columbia)
8th Battalion (90th Rifles)
10th Battalion

3rd Brigade

13th Battalion (Royal Highlanders)
14th Battalion (R. Montreal Regt.)
15th Battalion (48th Highlanders)
16th Battalion (Canadian Scottish)

Pioneers

1st Canadian Pioneer Battalion

2nd Canadian Division: Major General R.E.W. Turner

4th Brigade

18th (W. Ontario) Battalion
19th (Central Ontario) Battalion
20th (Central Ontario) Battalion
21st (Eastern Ontario) Battalion

5th Brigade

22nd (Canadien Français) Battalion
24th Battalion (Victoria Rifles)
25th Battalion (Nova Scotia Rifles)

26th (New Brunswick) Battalion

6th Brigade

27th Battalion (City of Winnipeg)
28th (North West) Battalion
29th (Vancouver) Battalion
31st (Alberta) Battalion

Pioneers

2nd Canadian Pioneer Battalion

3rd Canadian Division: Major General L.J. Lipsett

7th Brigade

Princess Patricia's Canadian LI
Royal Canadian Regt
42nd Battalion (Royal Highlanders)
49th (Edmonton) Battalion

8th Brigade

1st Canadian Mounted Rifles
2nd Canadian Mounted Rifles
3rd Canadian Mounted Rifles
4th Canadian Mounted Rifles

9th Brigade

43rd Battalion (Cameron Highlanders)
52nd (New Ontario) Battalion
58th Battalion
60th Battalion (Victoria Rifles)

Pioneers

3rd Canadian Pioneer Battalion

4th Canadian Division: Major General D. Watson

10th Brigade
44th Battalion
46th (S. Saskatchewan) Battalion
47th (British Columbia) Battalion
50th (Calgary) Battalion

11th Brigade
54th (Kootenay) Battalion
75th (Mississauga) Battalion
87th Battalion (Canadian Grenadier Guards)
102nd Battalion

12th Brigade
38th (Ottawa) Battalion
72nd Battalion (Seaforth Highlanders)
73rd Battalion (Royal Highlanders)
78th Battalion (Winnipeg Grenadiers)

Pioneers
67th Canadian Pioneer Battalion

New Zealand Division: Major General Sir A.H. Russell

1st New Zealand Brigade
1/Auckland
1/Canterbury
1/Otago
1/Wellington

2nd New Zealand Brigade
2/Auckland
2/Canterbury
2/Otago
2/Wellington

3rd New Zealand Rifle Brigade
1/New Zealand Brigade
2/New Zealand Brigade
3/New Zealand Brigade
4/New Zealand Brigade

Pioneers
New Zealand Pioneer Battalion

German Forces

3rd Guard Division
Guards Fus.
Lehr Regiment
Grenadier Regiment No. 9

4th Guard Division
5th Guards Foot
5th Guards Grenadiers
Reserve Regiment No. 93

5th Division
Grenadier Regiment Nos 8 and 12
Regiment No. 52

6th Division
Regiment Nos 30, 24 and 64

7th Division
Regiment Nos 26, 27 and 165

8th Division
Regiment Nos 72, 93 and 153

12th Division
Regiment Nos 23, 62 and 63

24th Division
Regiment Nos 133, 139 and 179

26th Division
Grenadier Regiment No. 119
Regiment Nos 121 and 125

27th Division
Regiment Nos 120, 124 and 127
Grenadier Regiment No. 123

38th Division
Regiment Nos 94, 95 and 96

40th Division
Regiment Nos 103, 134 and 181

52nd Division
Regiment Nos 66, 161 and 170

56th Division
Fusilier Regiment No. 35
Regiment Nos 88 and 118

58th Division
Regiment Nos 106 and 107
Reserve Regiment No. 120

111th Division
Fusilier Regiment No. 73
Regiment Nos 76 and 164

117th Division
Regiment No. 157
Reserve Regiment Nos 11 and 22

183rd Division
Regiment Nos 183 and 184
Reserve Regiment No. 122

185th Division
Regiment Nos 185, 186 and 190

208th Division
Regiment Nos 25 and 185
Reserve Regiment No. 65

222nd Division
Regiment Nos 193 and 397
Reserve Regiment No. 81

223nd Division
Regiment Nos 144 and 173
Ersatz Regiment No. 29

1st Guards Reserve Division
Guards Reserve Regiment Nos 1 and 2
Reserve Regiment No. 64

2nd Guards Reserve Division
Reserve Regiment Nos 15, 55, 77 and 91

7th Reserve Division
Reserve Regiment Nos 36, 66
and 72

12th Reserve Division
Reserve Regiment Nos 23, 38
and 51

17th Reserve Division
Regiment Nos 162 and 163
Reserve Regiment Nos 75 and
76

18th Reserve Division
Reserve Regiment Nos 31, 84
and 86

19th Reserve Division
Reserve Regiment Nos 73, 78,
79 and 92

23rd Reserve Division
Reserve Grenadier Regiment No.
101
Reserve Regiment Nos 101 and
102
Regiment No. 392

24th Reserve Division
Reserve Regiment Nos 101, 107
and 133

26th Reserve Division
Reserve Regiment Nos 99, 119
and 121
Regiment No. 180

28th Reserve Division
Reserve Regiment Nos 109, 110
and 111

45th Reserve Division
Reserve Regiment Nos 210, 211
and 212

50th Reserve Division
Reserve Regiment Nos 229, 230
and 231

51th Reserve Division
Reserve Regiment Nos 233, 234,
235 and 236

52nd Reserve Division
Reserve Regiment Nos 238, 239
and 240

4th Ersatz Division
Regiment Nos 359, 360, 361
and 362

5th Ersatz Division
Landwehr Regiment Nos 73 and
74
Reserve Landwehr Regiment
No. 3

2nd Bavarian Division
Bavarian Regiment Nos 12, 15
and 20

3rd Bavarian Division
Bavarian Regiment Nos 17, 18
and 23

4th Bavarian Division
Bavarian Regiment Nos 5 and 9
Bavarian Reserve Regiment No. 5

5th Bavarian Division
Bavarian Regiment Nos 7, 14, 19
and 21

6th Bavarian Division
Bavarian Regiment Nos 6, 10, 11
and 13

10th Bavarian Division
Bavarian Regiment No. 16
Bavarian Reserve Regiment Nos
6 and 8

6th Bavarian Reserve Division
Bavarian Reserve Regiment Nos
16, 17, 20 and 21

Bavarian Ersatz Division
Bavarian Reserve Regiment Nos
14 and 15
Ersatz Regiment No. 28

89th Reserve Brigade
Reserve Regiment Nos 209 and
213

Marine Brigade
Marine Regiment Nos 1, 2 and 3

FURTHER READING

Official History

Edmonds, Brigadier-General Sir James E., *Military Operations. France and Belgium, 1916: Sir Douglas Haig's Command to the 1st July: Battle of the Somme* (London: HMSO, 1932)

Edmonds, Brigadier-General Sir James E., *Military Operations. France and Belgium, 1916: Sir Douglas Haig's Command to the 1st July: Battle of the Somme, Appendices* (London: HMSO, 1932)

Edmonds, Brigadier-General Sir James E., *Military Operations. France and Belgium, 1916: 2nd July to the End of the Battle of the Somme* (London: HMSO, 1938)

James, Captain E.A., *A Record of the Battles and Engagements of the British Armies in France and Flanders, 1914–1918* (Aldershot: Gale & Polden, 1924; reprinted by The Naval and Military Press, Uckfield, n.d.)

General

Barton, Peter, *The Somme: A New Panoramic Perspective* (London: Constable, 2006)

Brown, Malcolm, *The Imperial War Museum Book of the Somme* (London: Pan, 1997)

Cuttell, Barry, *One Day on the Somme: 1st July 1916* (Peterborough: GMS Enterprises, 1998)

Cuttell, Barry, *158 Days on the Somme: 2nd July to 26th November 1916* (Peterborough: GMS Enterprises, 2000)

Farrar-Hockley, General Sir Anthony, *The Somme, Death of a Generation* (London: Batsford, 1964)

Gilbert, Martin, *Somme: The Heroism and Horror of War* (London: John Murray, 2006)

Gliddon, Gerald, *The Battle of the Somme: A Topographical History* (Stroud: Sutton, 1996)

MacDonald, Alan, *Pro Patria Mori: The 56th (1st London) Division at Gommecourt, 1st July 1916* (Liskeard: Diggory Press, 2006)

MacDonald, Alan, *'A Lack of Offensive Spirit?' The 46th (North Midland) Division at Gommecourt, 1st July 1916* (Liskeard: Diggory Press, 2008)

Macdonald, Lyn, *Somme* (London: Michael Joseph, 1983)

Masefield, John, *The Old Frontline* (Bourne End: Spurbooks Ltd, 1972)

Middlebrook, Martin, *The First Day on the Somme: 1 July 1916* (London: Allen Lane, 1971)

Middlebrook, Martin, *Your Country Needs You: Expansion of British Army Infantry Divisions, 1914–18* (Barnsley: Pen and Sword, 2000)

Pegler, Martin, *Attack on the Somme: Haig's Offensive 1916* (Barnsley: Pen and Sword, 2005)

Philpott, William, *Bloody Victory: The Sacrifice on the Somme and the Making of the Twentieth Century* (London: Little, Brown, 2009)

Robertshaw, Andrew, *Somme 1 July 1916, Tragedy and Triumph* (Oxford: Osprey, 2006)

Sheffield, Gary, *The Somme* (London: Cassell, 2003)

Biography

Bloem, Walter, *The Advance from Mons, 1914: The Experiences of a German Infantry Officer* (Solihull: Helion, 2004)

Crozier, Brigadier General F.P., *A Brass Hat in No Man's Land* (London: Jonathan Cape, 1930)

Jünger, Ernst, *The Storm of Steel: From the Diary of a German Storm-Troop Officer on the Western Front* (New York: Zimmermann & Zimmermann, 1985)

Malins, Lieutenant Geoffrey H. OBE, *How I Filmed the War* (London: Herbert Jenkens Ltd, 1920)

Maze, Paul, *A French Man in Khaki* (London: William Heinemann Ltd, 1936)

Sheffield, Gary and John Bourne (eds), *Douglas Haig: War Diaries and Letters 1914–1918* (London: Weidenfeld & Nicolson/BCA, 2005)

Sulzbach, Herbert, *With the German Guns: Four Years on the Western Front* (Barnsley: Pen and Sword, 1973)

Terraine, John (ed.), *General Jack's Diary 1914–1918: The Trench Diary of Brigadier-General J.L. Jack, D.S.O.* (London: Cassell and Co., 1964)

INDEX

Index